D1007454

Kilimanjaro

One Woman's Journey to the Roof of Africa and Beyond

ෲ৪৯

Kilimanjaro

ભ૪

One Woman's Journey
to the Roof of Africa
and Beyond

ભ૪

Deb Denis

Foreword by Simon Mtuy

*Tanzania's foremost trail runner, expert mountain
guide, and world record holder for the fastest
unsupported ascent and descent of Kilimanjaro*

MARION GRACE PUBLISHING
U.S.A.

Published in the United States by Marion Grace Publishing
Pennsylvania—U.S.A.
www.mariongracepublishing.com

First Edition: June 2012

ISBN 978-0-9857527-4-3 (Paperback)
ISBN 978-0-9857527-0-5 (Kindle)
ISBN 978-0-9857527-1-2 (EPUB)

For my family

TABLE OF CONTENTS

FOREWORD

As the 5th of 10 children born into a subsistence farm family in Marangu Mbahe Village, near the main entrance gate to Kilimanjaro National Park in Tanzania, education was scarce and opportunities were limited. After completing primary school and one year of secondary school I needed to work to earn income for my family and my future. Like many boys from the mountain with little formal education and few options I entered the climbing business, starting as a porter. At the age of 14 I began earning a few cents a day carrying huge loads of gear and equipment up the mountain for the tourists who came to climb Kilimanjaro. Despite the rigors of the hard physical labor, I enjoyed the excitement of being on the mountain, working as a team, and practicing English with the climbers. I saved my small wages for the guide training course and spent my free time learning as much as I could about the mountain. I finally submitted myself for the rigorous training entailing 6 days on the mountain, followed by 3 days of classroom lessons, and a final written exam in English. Upon completion, I became, at age 21, one of the youngest persons to earn my Kilimanjaro guide license. After a period of apprenticeship with other climb companies, in 1998 I registered my company and Summit Expeditions & Nomadic Experience (SENE) was born. From modest beginnings, SENE has prospered by abiding by the highest standards of comfort, health, safety, environmental ethics, and porter treatment.

As the owner of SENE and a mountain guide for two decades, I have seen thousands of people climb Mount Kilimanjaro. Yet during my 26 years of working on the mountain, I have rarely seen a woman climb the mountain as a solo climber, so I was very pleased when Deb chose us to be the outfitter and guide service for her incredible journey. As noted throughout this book, Deb faced many physical, psychological, and emotional challenges, but in the end she persevered and reached her goals while ascending to the *Roof of Africa*. As a non-athlete, Deb demonstrates that climbing Kilimanjaro is so much more than a mere physical challenge, but requires great emotional and spiritual fortitude. This resonates with me, as a Chagga child of the mountain who feels the immense spirit of Kilimanjaro every day.

We at SENE are proud that Deb chose Kilimanjaro for her personal adventure and that she was able to experience the thrill and excitement of the mountain with our team. While reading this book, you will enjoy the insights that Deb provides into the total climb experience. Often using humor, she describes the difficulty and serenity that comes with being disconnected from family yet connected to the mountain. She also provides helpful lessons learned from her experience that will allow future climbers to come to Kilimanjaro well-prepared—at multiple levels—for a successful summit.

I was delighted when Deb approached me about writing the foreword for her book because it shows to me that people who are serious about connecting with the mountain desire to share this experience with others. Many books about Kilimanjaro provide the reader with technical information about the routes, eco-zones, plants, animals, and climate on the mountain, but few authors have written about the experience on the mountain from the perspective of a solo climber (and none, that I am aware, who are women). I am honored that we at SENE could be a part of Deb's journey and thankful for her willingness to encourage others in their personal aspirations. You too will find inspiration and delight in her insights. Asante sana Deb!

Kila la heri (all the best),

Simon Mtuy

Founder and Senior Guide
Summit Expeditions & Nomadic Experience
Kilimanjaro, Moshi, Tanzania

Author's Preface: About the Book

This book combines multiple types of media: typed excerpts from the handwritten journal I kept in the beginning, until I lost three pens—two of my own and one borrowed—as well as transcripts from recordings I made during the climb. These appear in italics to highlight what was actually from the journal and recordings. I've included quoted sections (also italicized) from the itinerary provided by the company that guided me up the mountain. Throughout the book, I've also interspersed quotes from other people who have been inspirational to me, because they just seem to fit here.

I created a website to go with the book, www.HerSoloSummit.com, where you'll find some of the actual recordings—my way to share with you the spontaneous emotion of particular moments. When I wasn't focused on breathing, walking slowly and drinking water, I was talking to my guides about the landscape and taking pictures, which you'll also see on the website. On many of the later days of the climb I took short videos at camp, which I shared with family and friends when I got home. Their enthusiastic responses to this media convinced me the videos needed to be included, so it's all available to you on the website.

By seeing and hearing my story through the recordings, the pictures and the videos on the website, I hope you'll get a sense of what this experience was like. Come along on the adventure with me . . . .

*   *   *

There are several audiences for this book: those who have said yes to a Kilimanjaro climb and have already done it, or are just about to; those who are interested in and may be considering a Kilimanjaro climb in the future; and those who can't imagine they ever would or could climb this mountain, but who may be inspired to try this or some other big, crazy goal. This book is also for people who are simply interested in reading a true story of adventure.

If you're in the have/will/may climb group, you'll find the research components of this book helpful—the steps I took to narrow down the sea of choices surrounding the climb that you've undoubtedly encountered already. For those in the group of "I can't imagine myself doing [insert your intimidating goal here]," I hope you'll be inspired by the story and find yourself establishing your own crazy goal to accomplish.

This book is also about what I learned and how I grew through the experience of being in East Africa for a month, which included giving myself permission to leave, and incorporating the lessons learned there after coming home.

To me, this climb was a big goal that delivered big lessons. I share it all with you, the reader, since, though these are my experiences, each of you has your own challenges to work through and maybe, just maybe, part of this story will resonate with yours.

Kilimanjaro

ೞ

One Woman's Journey to the Roof of Africa
and Beyond

PROLOGUE

My name is Deb Denis and when I was 45 years old, I decided I wanted to climb Mt. Kilimanjaro before I turned 50. This is the story of that journey.

From my online Journal on June 1st—Departure Day

What is the name of that game where the dealer holds up the cards and says, "Pick a card, any card"? That's been the theme of the past week for me . . . with emotions. Pick an emotion, any emotion, and I have it going on.

A little homesick already but too juiced up on adrenaline and lots to do before I sleep. Up at 4 a.m., going, going, going until 11 p.m. when I set the alarm for 2 a.m. and give it a try . . . tossing, turning, sleeping for a short time, then waiting for the alarm to ring, which it does.

I am packed, ready as I'll be for this adventure, and so very excited for it to begin. For weeks it's been sharing the mental and emotional plate with so many other worries but it's time to go. My ride should be here any minute.

Eighteen minutes later she's not here, so I call. "Michelle, where are you?" A sleepy voice tells me this business owner of an airport transport company forgot about me, but there's no time to be crushed about it . . . got to go! Now it's time to pull a rabbit out of the hat: "I've got to call a cab!" I tell her, hanging up.

I make it to the airport late but strangely on time . . . the gate doesn't open for another 20 minutes.

Ah, it's a great feeling to be early to the airport and confident that I'm as ready as I can be, bags are so efficiently packed that Chip—our son who is prepared for everything—and my husband Alan—the packing efficiency expert—would be impressed.

The check-in gate finally opens, but the self-directed check-in kiosk can't find me. An agent discovers the problem—I'm flying

1

tomorrow. Ah, it's great to be early at the airport . . . but this early? Flooded with embarrassment—did I actually just go through all of yesterday's craziness a day early? I catch another cab and go home. It's an expensive mistake but on the way home I think about it.

There isn't anything to do. I'm ready, the house is ready, everyone believes I'm flying to Africa today . . . heck, so did I until less than an hour ago. So, what should I do today?

Driving back home at 4:30 a.m., the sky begins its transition, providing just enough light to see homes along the way. They're idyllic in their stillness—different homes, different families all nestled inside and sleeping soundly. I breathe deeper to enjoy wafts of summer blossoms. I do love this place we call home.

BECOMING A LIGHTER PRESENCE IN THE WORLD

Walking on the edge is where she grows.

The whole idea of climbing Mt. Kilimanjaro started to form when I was in Paris with a group of international accounting practitioners. Two men previously with the group had attempted the climb a year before; one of them made it to the top, the other became sick from the altitude and did not. I'd never known anyone who'd climbed Mt. Kilimanjaro, at least not that I knew of. It never would have entered my mind to do something like that.

I left the conference and travelled to Asheville, North Carolina, for a professional development retreat. I'm an Executive Coach by training and trade, and a self-declared lifelong learner. They say that when you love what you do it's not work, and I love being and growing as a Coach.

At the end of the presence-based coaching retreat, I made a commitment to "being a lighter presence in the world." I didn't know *exactly* what it meant but had a general idea that it consisted of three parts: lighter, presence, and world.

To meet the objective of being lighter, I thought my plan should include the kinds of activities that would help me be more flexible and move more freely, like yoga. I could be lighter physically by losing weight. I could approach the world with a lighter, less uptight presence, one that could be cultivated through meditation. Think Buddhist without a lot of rules.

I wanted a healthy, thinner body; a less scattered, more ordered mind; and a resulting energy that would extend into the world through my coaching. I wanted other people to experience me as a calm, centered presence. Yoga, meditation and exercise would surely contribute to developing me into a person with a grounded, satisfied, and pleasant presence. Think Zen.

This is what it means to be a lighter presence in the world.

3

The conversation in Paris had obviously stuck in my head somewhere, because climbing Mt. Kilimanjaro seemed just big enough and far-out enough to be the concrete goal that would help me focus on being lighter mentally, physically and emotionally. It seemed like an inspirational goal to me and, since I was only 45, I figured I would have years to work on the details.

In the nearer term, my world was dark, and my heart heavier than it had ever been. One month before the retreat, I was told that my mom had a malignant brain tumor, a glioblastoma. When I looked it up, I found the survival rate was zero beyond three years for her age group. What I didn't know at the time was that her doctor had told her it would probably be much less time for her. Feeling weighted down by hopelessness, I desperately wanted and needed to be a lighter presence in the world, so I could support her and survive this myself.

In North Carolina, in a small circle of colleagues from around the globe, I declared my commitment to being a lighter presence in the world, and to the goal of climbing Mt. Kilimanjaro before I turned 50. Yoga, meditation, diet, exercise, and dealing with difficult emotions (mine and others) would certainly soothe my despondency. By doing all of this development work, I would certainly become that lightness of being who would zen-float up the mountain a few years from now.

This was an aggressive goal and the fact that it was vague flew completely counter to what I advise my clients, who only get to work on one thing at a time. Focus, I tell them, will help to ensure that you achieve your goals—one at a time. Otherwise, your energy is diffused, scattered to the winds, and chances are you'll accomplish little over the long haul. I'm a smart cookie and a good coach. Why then, was I not listening to my own advice?

There was work to be done on many levels here. On the physical level, I was about 15 pounds overweight according to the high end of the Weight Watchers scale. I was strong, but certainly not in any shape for mountain climbing—we've hiked as a family for over ten years, so I know what it takes to keep up and I wasn't there. Earlier in the year, I'd worked with a dynamo nutritionist, Ali Shapiro, on an extended 28-day cleanse during which I had no caffeine, no alcohol, no dairy, no sugar, no wine and no processed foods for 28 days straight . . . not for sissies, I'm telling you. There would certainly be a few more of those in my future.

Mentally and emotionally, I was operating on a few different planes, all at once. I was relieved to be wrapping up the retreat and returning home. I had made a commitment to extend my coaching work into the world and looked forward to new professional objectives.

Rushing beneath it all was the undertow of what was happening at home. Not surprisingly, the strong emotional current of it regularly pulled my mind under, making it difficult to focus on anything else. Fortunately, the climb was years away from actually happening, so there was no pressure. But, I believed that the goal of a climb would inspire me to get busy physically, which would provide the added benefit of mental and emotional stress relief.

When I came home from North Carolina, I didn't feel like focusing on any of it. The family dynamic was intense and I was tossed around by waves of emotion, both old and new.

*   *   *

Psychologists often focus on issues stemming from a person's family of origin, since family dynamics are rarely, if ever, confined to a single time or place. In telling this story, I mention my family; its tree is splintered, which makes the relationships confusing and complicated. Knowing some of the history will provide insight into what I brought along with me, emotionally, on this journey. The fractured nature of my family informed decisions I made and emotions I struggled with. Although my family has often been a great source of strength for me, it has sometimes been a maelstrom for me to escape from.

My family drama began with my parents' divorce in 1969 when I was four and my sister Karen was two. After a short time struggling as a single parent, our mother relinquished custody to our father. His job moved to upstate New York and we went with it. My mother remarried a few years later and started a new family; my sister Jennifer was born in 1975 and twins George and David in 1976. Even as a child, I sensed her husband didn't like me very much. Many years later, I asked my mother about it and she told me that I was a reminder to him that she'd been married before. My father also remarried, twice in fact, before I was 18.

Karen and I visited Philadelphia every summer, staying with our maternal grandparents and visiting with Mom, when she had time off from work, along with her husband George and their kids. The visits were always too short; leaving was always gut-wrenching. One summer, I think it was before Jennifer was born, Mom gave Karen and me each a girl's necklace with a small cloisonné "bluebird of happiness" charm on it. She told us it was to remind us to be happy even when we felt sad. I lost that necklace; I can't remember when. Summer would always come to an end too soon, and Karen and I were like little puddles every year when it was time to leave. George asked us once if we could try not to cry so much when we left because it upset our mother. We tried, but we just couldn't help it. I still cry when I leave a place that's touched me deeply, or when I leave my sister, Karen, at the airport. Old habits.

I loved school, was an accomplished student and was socially agile. I earned money by babysitting, and in high school I rode my bike on busy roads after school and on the weekends to get to work at a retail store in the mall.

But I was a handful. I would go dancing with girlfriends in the clubs until the wee hours and was interested in boys, normal teenage antics, actually. I could have been much worse. Nonetheless, in my role as oldest child, I presented a "first time" challenge to all of my parents. In fact, my father declared that his responsibilities to raise me had been met after I'd turned 18 and graduated from high school. After that, he didn't speak to me for ten years.

To all of my parental units, I say, "Sorry I was tough to manage."

My maternal grandparents came to my high school graduation along with the family I babysat for. The next day my grandparents brought me to live with them in Philadelphia. My Gram was the best; she taught me about unconditional love.

I got a job. The next part of life began.

Fast-forward a dozen years and this headstrong wild child met the man of her dreams. Thank goodness I am married to an intelligent, even-tempered (and very handsome) man, Alan, who loves life and who—importantly—appreciates strong, smart women. His cool logic is the ideal foil for my warm-to-hot reactions. This would become even more important as the family, and especially I, faced my mother's cancer. Alan hadn't been swimming in the same family pool as I; he could see more clearly and helped me do the same, whenever he could. He was my life preserver.

*   *   *

Lines were drawn when Mom was diagnosed. Lightly at first and then with more emphasis, it was made clear that her husband, and in his absence, Jennifer (his oldest child), would make all the medical decisions and speak for Mom. My mother asked me to understand, to let it be, because it would be easier that way.

My ideas, suggestions, thoughts, and connections to doctors and others—professionals at Penn, in healthcare, in bioPharma—none of them mattered, was welcomed or considered helpful. Quite the opposite, in fact; I was forbidden to speak to her doctors and was told on more than one occasion not to ask "stupid questions." Being a lightning rod is one of my special gifts.

As you might expect, I resisted, but that only made the situation worse; they closed ranks around her. Subterfuge was useless, as was sharing anything I'd learned through research or from the experience and expertise of others. Asking questions put others on defense. I asked questions from my own desire to understand, which was tolerated, but only for a short time. The old family fractures created collateral damage—to my ego and my heart. I struggled to understand, rationalize, accept and comply with each new rule declared, or boundary established. I told myself, maybe that's just the way it is.

At one point my husband said, "the most important question is this: is your mother getting the best possible care?" My immediate answer was "Maybe, I don't know," since there still seemed to be room left for some other possibility. What about better treatment, even something experimental, or another opinion, or the world's expert—this was for my mother and I would have gone to the ends of the earth to find what she needed. But that's what *I* wanted to do. And what mattered now was what my mother wanted. The truth for my mom was that she did have all that she needed, she was well cared for, and the very best thing I could do was to back off. So I tried.

*   *   *

Just because one part of your life is a complete mess doesn't mean the other parts of life stop; quite the contrary, they demand equal if not more attention. I had Alan at home, our sons, Chip and Mike, living in different places, and I had my work—all needing my care and attention. Work was a welcome focus; as something I did well and was appreciated for, it nourished my wounded ego and soul.

Two weeks after returning home from the North Carolina retreat, I had a Saturday afternoon call scheduled with Heidrun, a coaching colleague I'd met during our distance-learning professional coaching certification studies. We'd been working together, virtually, via the Internet, for well over a year and the formal conversations were nearing an end, which made me sad.

Heidrun is someone I admire. She does good work in the world and she, like me, loves coaching and learning. She is disciplined in ways that astound me—with her meditation practice and diet; oh, and she speaks six languages and continues to learn more of them. I wanted to find a way to maintain the connection; Heidrun did, too. We each brought to that Saturday morning call our own ideas to keep the conversations going. My idea was Coaches Without Borders (you can read about it here: www.coaches-without-borders.org). Heidrun's idea was that I should join her for a leadership summit in Burundi in the spring.

To me, the world is a small place where all you need is a passport and a plane ticket to experience another culture; I love to travel. I should also tell you that though we'd been working together for over a year, I'd never seen a picture of Heidrun, not even a video-picture via Skype or a photo on the Internet. I had no idea where Burundi was, but it didn't matter. The chance to work with Heidrun anywhere in Africa would be marvelous and I said "Yes!" right away.

Seeing the potential of so many possibilities thrilled me! I had a lot of ideas and content to offer in support of the conference, since it was what I'd been doing and teaching for a few years now. Heidrun liked the idea of Coaches Without Borders, and we agreed to pilot it. The next steps were for me to write up our combined ideas in a way that Heidrun could use as a proposal within her organization. Before I got to work on the write-up, however, I wanted to understand where on the continent Burundi was. So, after finishing the call, I Googled "Burundi."

Burundi is the smallest African country, completely landlocked and bordered by the Democratic Republic of Congo to the west, Rwanda to the north and Tanzania to the east and south. I

9

couldn't believe what I was seeing . . . can you guess what's in Tanzania?

If you guessed Mt. Kilimanjaro, then you win the prize—and that's exactly how I felt, like I'd just won a prize package composed of work I know and love, with someone I have incredible admiration and respect for, in Africa(!), and within very close proximity of Mt. Kilimanjaro. The hairs on my arms stood up. My pulse quickened. My eyebrows rose up in disbelief, while the corners of my mouth also rose up, into a smile that wouldn't leave my face.

It was just two short weeks ago that I'd expressed my intention to climb Mt. Kilimanjaro. I thought it would be years away. Yet here it was, right in my lap, as if the universe responded to my request to climb the mountain by saying, "Okay, you asked for it so I'm bringing it within reach. Now, what will you do with this opportunity?"

That little bit of research to locate Burundi on the map turned into a whole lot of research into what it would take to prepare to climb Mt. Kilimanjaro. It was June 2010 and I couldn't quite believe it: I would be travelling to Africa in the spring of 2011.

The prospect of this was energizing, but what if it didn't really happen? The truth was, for many months, I didn't *actually* believe that it would or could happen. I couldn't let my hopes get too set on it and risk being crushed. With all that was happening with Mom, I could only focus on one day at a time; I didn't want to think too far into the future about that. So, although I jumped into the planning process for all three big projects with gusto—Coaches Without Borders, the Leadership Conference in Burundi, and Kilimanjaro—the idea of actually going to Africa remained surreal.

I listened to Alan's advice and didn't let myself become too emotionally invested in it happening until the dates were set. Meanwhile, I both appreciated and enjoyed the chance to focus on such exciting projects; they kept my mind busy and I needed that.

TRAIL MAP FOR MT. KILIMANJARO

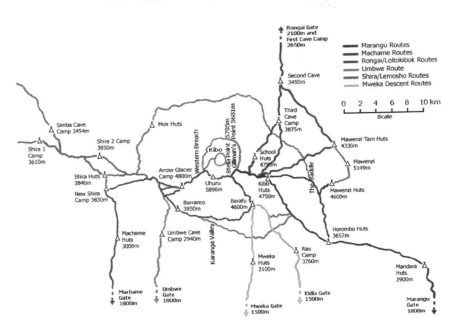

Used with permission from www.frontiersoftravel.com

I had never done such extensive research for a trip before—that's usually Alan's department. With several months to research and prepare, I looked online, read books, and tracked key criteria on spreadsheets. Henry Stedman's book on Kilimanjaro was my encyclopedia. From it, I learned what to consider, and what to look for, to determine which route to take, and which company to hire to take me there. If you're considering a Kilimanjaro climb, I've included the details of my research and thought process in the Appendix at the end of this book.

Some decisions were easy to make, while others took time. I didn't know the dates of the Burundi conference yet, so that created an open jaw in the planning process. However, I did know after a small amount of research which route I wanted to take.

11

People die on the mountain, several each year in fact. They die from heart attacks, severe altitude sickness, falls and avalanches. One route was labeled as the most dangerous in comparison to the others, especially since January 2006, when three trekkers were killed by rock that broke loose, and fell from the base of a glacier on the face of the mountain. They were on this most dangerous route. For several years after that incident, the route was closed while studies were done to evaluate if and when it would ever be opened up again.

The trail has since been reopened. However, most Kilimanjaro companies won't even consider taking clients on this route, and extreme caution is advised.

The official report indicates "The r-shaped glacier from which the rocks fell in January 2006 continues to recede and to release more rocks . . . the route remains prone to rock fall in at least three places. Each of these "kill zones" can be crossed quickly, minimizing exposure to risk, however it is of course possible that rock fall can impact a climber even while crossing these small zones quickly.[1]

Yes, the route was and still is dangerous. In fact, less than ten percent of Kilimanjaro climbers choose this route, but it was the one that sparkled most *for me,* for several reasons.

First, it was the route less travelled and that appealed to me because I enjoy peace and quiet when I hike. I don't like to be behind or around talkers or other people in general. I appreciate space to clear my mind when I'm on the trail; to me, that is one of the alluring facets of hiking, along with exercise and being in nature.

Second, this struck me as the most efficient route, by far. My research indicated that on this route, unlike any other, you get to sleep in the crater of the volcano at 18,800 feet, and that to me

---

[1] www.westernbreach.co.uk/route.html for a conservative perspective on this route

was a very shiny prospect. Stedman's book indicated it was possible to feel the ground warm to the touch at certain spots within the crater. The volcanic dust is soft to sleep in. There are glaciers! Yes, it was dangerous, but the idea of sleeping in the crater was irresistible.

Plus, sleeping in the crater puts you just 90 minutes away from the summit the next morning, a bonus when you consider the other routes have trekkers waking up in the very early hours of the morning, walking the long way uphill to make it to the summit, only to immediately walk back down. I wanted to enjoy the summit, not be wiped out getting there.

It seemed to me the 90-minute trek to the summit was the most efficient AND the best approach, since I didn't know how I'd respond to hours-long treks in the higher altitudes. This certainly seemed like the route for me.

One Tanzanian guide company actually specializes in this route; they actually offer two different paths that include sleeping in the crater. Here is a summary from Summit Expeditions and Nomadic Experiences (SENE). Which approach would you choose?

"This is our most popular itinerary for its beauty, 9 total days on the mountain (for maximum acclimatization), and the excitement of spending an overnight at 18,800 feet inside the crater on Kilimanjaro. The route takes us from the west across the Shira Plateau, with an ascent to the base of the Lava Tower, which you will be able to climb for magnificent 360 degree vistas. From Lava Tower there are two approaches to the crater and summit. Groups will have discussed and decided upon their choice during their climb preparations in Mbahe. One approach is from the southwest through the Western Breach, the classic route to the crater with a challenging rock scramble done in the early morning. The other is a longer and less steep approach from Barafu, farther east, and offering the opportunity of summiting twice. After the overnight camped in the soft sand of the crater, we have a sunrise climb to Uhuru Peak before descending toward

the southeast and incredible views of Mawenzi, Kilimanjaro's remnant volcanic cone."

Challenging and steep did it for me; I picked the rock scramble up to the western breach of the crater.

*   *   *

Two men are sitting at the dinner table, father and son, and someone is missing.

"Have you heard anything from her?" one asks.

"No, haven't heard anything yet."

"What do you think the odds are that she'll make it?"

Both men agree to write their guesses down on separate pieces of paper, and then compare their answers. One gives her a 50% chance, the other, even less.

I was not happy when I first heard this story. In fact, I was offended at how little faith these men had in me. After some time to reflect, however, I remembered that there is often a grain of truth in what might appear on its face to be an insult. Not always, but sometimes, and it's an opportunity for me to try to see a situation from the other person's perspective.

When I was finished being miffed by this scene, I realized that in this case, statistics[2] would prove both men right: only 40 to 50 percent of people who attempt to climb this mountain actually make it all the way to the summit. I was determined to be one of them.

---

[2] I found varying numbers based on my online research and in books. The guide services will tell you what their success rates are, and when they're published by service, you'll find them in the high 80s and 90s. Other overall mountain statistics I found indicated that, on the whole, only 40% to 50% of all climbers reach the summit.

Determination isn't enough, though. Neither is endurance or strength. It's just not that simple when you're up against Mother Nature. Martina Navratolova, unarguably one of the world's most accomplished athletes, did not make it to the summit. Guides and porters who climb this mountain for a living can still be sickened by the altitude and have to be carried down, sometimes flown out via helicopter, if it's severe. Young or old, every person can, at high altitude, be hit by Acute Mountain Sickness (AMS), a.k.a. altitude sickness, or its nasty relatives, pulmonary or cerebral edema.

Lower amounts of oxygen and lower air pressure combine at higher altitudes to produce bodily responses of dizziness, light-headedness, raging headaches, and a loss of appetite. In the danger zone, you could feel symptoms like a tight chest, shortness of breath, congestion, coughing, even an inability to walk a straight line—or walk at all. For some, AMS is fatal.

*　　*　　*

The altitude of Kilimanjaro intimidated me more than any other aspect of the climb. Yes, I was (and still am) out of top shape, but my legs are strong and I'd been hiking with my husband, Alan, and our sons, Chip and Mike, for the ten years we've been a family, so I believed that I had the physical strength to do it.

I believed that altitude and attitude were most likely to be my obstacles.

I'd been dizzy on fast ascents before. The first time was driving to Aspen, Colorado when, near the top of Independence Pass, elevation 12,095 feet (3687 meters), I got the dizzies big time and didn't at first realize what it was. It happened again when we had an opportunity to go glacier hiking in Zermatt, Switzerland, on the Klein Matterhorn, elevation 12,780 feet (3885 meters). Despite a week of acclimatization in Zermatt, hiking around the mountain and climbing up and down the considerable hill to our house for the week, I felt dizzy near the top of the Matterhorn. So, my history was dizziness above 12,000 feet, and I was contemplating climbing to 19,340 feet. Could I do it?

I wanted to give myself every advantage possible, within reason. I learned from my research that the more time on the trail, the better the acclimatization. The longer the trek, the more likely I was to adapt to the altitude. My dizziness in Aspen's Independence Pass and Switzerland's Matterhorn both occurred after rapid ascents by car and ski-lift, whereas Kilimanjaro would be *en pied*, on foot: walking in. My list of preferences was growing. I wanted to take the Western Breach route, explore and camp in the crater, and I wanted as long a trek as reasonably possible.

A lot of reading plus multiple international telephone calls and emails over the next few months helped me decide which company to go with, which wasn't easy because there are literally hundreds of companies to choose from. For me, my goals, my itinerary, and my schedule, the best company was SENE; if you want to know more about why they were my choice, check out the Appendix at the end of this book.

*   *   *

The reaction I typically got when I mentioned the impending trip was, "Are you nuts?" Those who'd climbed before, though, were excited to share what they knew. One dinner guest told me that if I could walk the gauntlet (the rotating steps at the gym) at level six, for 60 uninterrupted minutes, that I'd be okay on Kilimanjaro.

I was careful about what I said and shared with family, about my planning for Africa, because they all had so much on their minds. We had no idea what would happen with Mom and just took it day by day. Friends who were tuned in to what was happening were supportive and encouraging. Mostly, the planning for

Africa was a private project. Until the dates were set for the conference in Burundi it remained surreal, like a dream that might come true, but wasn't completely assured.

My husband was less than thrilled that his wife wanted to spend a month in Africa, working in Burundi, and attempting a dangerous summit. And did I mention that I wanted to see the Great Migration in the Serengeti? It's right there on the map, spanning Tanzania and Kenya. If the herds would be within striking distance, then I knew I had to try to see them. When would I ever be back in East Africa? Maybe never. If you've ever seen the National Geographic special, *The Great Migration,* narrated by James Earl Jones, then you know what I mean when I say it was too great to resist or to miss.

I kept on researching and planning and waiting for the date to be set for Burundi, which would determine the rest of the dates for the trip. I knew the conference would be held in the spring but wasn't sure if it would be March, or April, or May. Once the dates were set—for late May 2011—it was a lot tougher not to talk about it over the dinner table because *now it was real.*

All of a sudden, it seemed there were news stories every week about tourists being kidnapped in Kenya. I booked my flights. Alan brought to my attention newspaper articles of more tourist kidnappings and murders in East Africa. I signed the contract with the climbing company. Alan insisted I register my itinerary with the U.S. State Department, which I did. I didn't share the travel warnings I received from them via email, confident that I would be in good hands with my in-Africa hosts. I reviewed every detail of the 15-page security briefing prepared by the Security Officer in Burundi and kept on meeting with the planning committee to prepare for the work to be done there.

And, I kept on scheduling time to see my mom when it fit with the family roster. Continuing to insert myself into the family so that I could spend time with Mom was sort of like giving blood: after donating a few gallons you develop so much scar tissue that it starts to show on the surface.

In my life, when I've felt dead on the inside, it's not been unusual for me to plan something outrageous and crazy; it reminds me that I'm alive.

IT'S TIME TO GO, OR, IS IT?

The family dynamic surrounding my mother's battle against a foe that would not be defeated continued to swirl, pulling us all into its depths, but none more strongly than my mom. Since being diagnosed with the brain tumor in May 2010, she'd had radiation and chemotherapy and three neurosurgeries. Each surgery left her progressively depleted, physically and mentally, knocking her back to almost zero each time. She endured month after month of grueling therapies—physical, speech, occupational—to rebuild her abilities as much as possible. She was given steroids to reduce the swelling, which made her paranoid; she was often fearful for her life while she was staying in the rehabilitation facility. It was agonizing to know this happened to her night after night, but her husband and daughter Jennifer were always a phone call away and the twins were too. My number wasn't on anybody's list.

If I sound bitter, I was. This was the saddest experience of my life. I know everyone was frustrated, as we all felt helpless in the face of what Mom endured. Still, I wanted to count. I wanted to matter. I wanted to be there when she had bad dreams, to hug her and tell her that they were just bad dreams. I wanted to do something helpful. I wished that I could have been more helpful. But it wasn't about me or what I wanted, after all; it was about Mom.

On the days I was with her in rehab, I was in awe and so proud of how hard she worked, while at the same time I was choked by the collar of not being allowed to ask questions or speak to anyone about her treatment. I wasn't able to answer simple questions the nursing staff would ask without calling Jennifer; it was embarrassing and frustrating. I felt stupid and useless. I felt like crying that my mother had to endure this, and I couldn't do very much of anything to make it better. None of us could.

By late May of 2011, a year after her original diagnosis, she'd been through hell and back more than a couple of times and had made the decision to let the tumor take its course naturally, and to receive hospice care, without any more surgery. She and her husband moved in with Jennifer, which allowed them to be closer to the hospital and doctors' offices.

During several of my visits leading up to the month in Africa, Mom and I had conversations about whether I should or would go. We agreed that her care was covered, that she had what she needed. She told me emphatically that she did not want me to cancel the trip.

"And if I die while you're gone, I do not want you to change the plan and come home early. What good would it do for you to come home? I'll already be dead!"

She meant it. And in a twisted way, it made sense because my being there was useless. I desperately wished that this wasn't true but, in fact, everyone was better off and it was more peaceful for Mom as a result, when I wasn't in the mix. It was a brutal decision to make but it was time to go forward as planned, albeit woefully.

Fast-forward—just days to go now.

I wish I could tell you that I'd accomplished all of the preliminary goals I had set: to meditate, do yoga, have a better diet, eliminate caffeine and wine for the month before I left to cleanse my system, lose 20 pounds, work out, be super-strong and super-thin and have less weight to carry up that mountain. But I didn't hit those targets. My energy just wasn't in it. My heart was heavy and so was I, having added another 13 pounds to my frame (when did that happen?). I did accomplish the goal of a full, uninterrupted hour on the stair-stepping gauntlet at level six, but it was incredibly boring and so, after hitting that target once, I gave myself permission to change it up. I still made it to the gym several days a week, every week, but there were days when I felt so overwhelmed by it all—I had to just let it out and cry a few tears while climbing or running or stepping or just walking.

Tim, at SENE, sent me a long email with "last minute details," which I forwarded to my husband, Alan and sister, Karen, along with my full itinerary and the contact information for the various

U.K., U.S. and African contacts who would be able to reach me in-country. I sent all of the same to my colleague, Linda DeLuca, and to Alan's assistant, Kristin, just in case.

The last two times I saw my mom before I left were to celebrate her birthday and to have some quiet just-her-and-me time. The birthday party included family and "friends who are family;" we all sat out back on my sister's screened-in porch, enjoying the sunshine and nice weather. My nephew, a seven-year-old budding artist, alternated between Mom-Mom's lap and mine, and drew a picture "For Ant Deb." He was learning to draw cartoon images and mine had a bubble saying "Hi, I'm Ant Deb and I like to go on Adventures." At the top it's signed, "Love, Georgie." I treasured this picture because it reminded me that someone in the family loved me at a time when I wasn't feeling much love there. I brought it with me to Africa.

*   *   *

The clock is ticking and now there are ***just 48 hours to go* . . . .**

Alan had left for business in Mexico just a few days before. The house was quiet, as clean as it would be. I had one final work project to deliver, a webinar on coaching. The mental checklists were on continuous loop. What else did I need to do before leaving home for a month? T-minus-2-days and counting . . . .

My son Chip and I had dinner at the local burger pub; I was excited, distracted, running on nervous energy and could barely eat. Driving home, my car got a flat tire. We changed it in the fading light of day and were aided by a passerby with a pickup truck who stopped, and shone his headlights for us to see.

It was during the tire changing that I realized I'd missed a detail: the plan was for Jennifer to call Karen if anything happened with Mom. Then Karen would call Alan, and then she'd fly here (from Florida to Pennsylvania) and use my house and car. One of them, Karen or Alan, would call me.

[From Email] *To Karen, cc: Chip – May 30, 2011, 9:17p.m.*

Hi—flat tire tonight and Chip saved the day (thank you Chip!)

We realized that Alan will be in Mexico, then home, then in China. What if you call and he's travelling? So, Chip is your next call. He knows where the house key is, and can coordinate with you if need be while I'm gone. He knows where I'm leaving the car keys and how everything works in the house. So you'll be in very good hands either way.

Ciao for now, Deb

*   *   *

24 hours to go . . . .

[From my online journal] *May 31ˢᵗ: Today my mom told me that she believes she'll still be here when I get back. The steroids are giving her energy, even more use of her right arm and hand, and I believe her because I can see the difference and agree. Her speech and cognition seem better too. Choosing to say, "See you when I get back, see you in July," is so much easier on the heart than saying a last good bye.*

My mother has given me so many gifts—"we come from strong stock" she told me last week—and I believe I just received another one.

*   *   *

The night before it was time to leave I triple-checked my bags, laid out my clothes for the next day and set the alarm clock. Nervous excitement and exhaustion combined to fog up my mind, yet I was barely able to sleep. Feeling like a zombie, I stared at the clock, and then closed my eyes.

You know how this part of the story goes: I woke up before the alarm clock and made it to the airport, only to learn that my flight wasn't actually scheduled to leave until the next day. So I and my luggage made our way, from the departures section of the airport, all the way over to baggage/arrivals where the taxi stand is, and got into a cab to go back home.

[From Online Journal] *As soon as I got home I sent an email to Michelle, the owner of the airport driving service, to apologize for waking her up and for my mistake.*

Beyond contacting Michelle, I decided I wouldn't tell anyone about this day-early mistake—it was so embarrassing, and for what purpose? So my husband could worry? Though the first

23

instinct was to avoid embarrassment, reflection gave me a sense of peace to simply, quietly, and privately enjoy the day.

Resisting the urge to "do" is tough. Today I'll play with that.

I noticed some chafing around my ankles so the first outing was to the shoemaker in Newtown Square, to have my hiking boots softened around the ankles. Comfortable, broken-in boots are crucial for this journey and I wondered if maybe this was the whole reason I had this gift of a day. But the old, traditional shoemaker's shop was closed, a Great Harvest Bread Company in its place, and I felt sad at the loss of a good local shop. Inquiring in the bread company, I learned that the shoemaker may have returned to Russia, and one of the patrons there recommended a shoe shop in Wayne. One door closes, and another one opens, so it was off to Wayne for me.

Hazy, hot and humid visited Philly early this year, but the cool front left behind a perfect day today. Leisurely driving for a few errands that could have waited, but now don't have to, I'm again reminded of how much I love this place. The smell of freshly mown grass; quaint downtown Wayne, which always reminds me of Spring Lake, NJ, a favorite getaway place; the wind moving gentle patterns in the long golden grasses; the black angus cows taking their leisure in the rich, green grass, enjoying a generously shaded spot for siesta. Colors are more vivid on a day like today—the bursting yellow blooms blast out against the deep green grasses, all under a robin's egg light blue. I love how every wrong turn today has led me to something else—finding an ATM on the way, and the CVS. And the shoe repair shop is just what I needed. They pounded the stiff leather around the ankle of each boot so I'm truly good to go.

*So many gifts in just one day and there's a lot to be grateful for— now **this** is the attitude and energy to have for an African adventure. I often say, "We get what we need when we need it" and today, I have.*

That evening, I enjoyed sitting outside on the deck in the early summer air, appreciating life. Alan was working in Mexico, my pup Athena was staying with her trainer in his house, with his dogs for company. Mom had seemed strong and on an upswing, improving. It was quiet, peaceful. My sister Karen called to wish me a safe journey; she's the one who's adept at details and knew that I wasn't actually leaving until the next day. I told her about the early trip to the airport (I tell her everything) and we chuckled.

This time, I got more sleep and was up and ready to go early the next morning. I checked my bags again and gave myself an imaginary pat on the back, knowing with certainty that Alan and the boys would be impressed with how efficiently those bags were packed.

Peacefulness and gratitude had replaced adrenaline; I arrived at the airport with the confidence of a pro who'd made this trip before.

*   *   *

Instead of berating myself for the royal mix-up, I reflected on the gifts of the day, and gave myself permission to let the embarrassment go; that was comforting. Looking back on this time I can see that I was at my best when I focused with a grateful eye on the present moment, a perspective I adopted as a survival technique, I believe. I didn't want to look back, since looking back meant grappling with emotional memories that intertwined like a riptide with the strength to pull me under. I didn't want to think too far into the future, didn't want to see that place in time when I would have to acknowledge the reality of the inevitable regarding Mom. Avoiding thoughts of the past and future wore me out because I couldn't in actuality avoid them . . . they were always there. It was exhausting. Life was easier when I focused on what was directly and immediately in front of me, right here, right now.

I looked forward to the adventure, to a change of scenery, to doing good work in Burundi. I gently pushed aside sadness about home or nervousness about Kilimanjaro and instead, thought about the work immediately ahead in Burundi. It was time to get onto the plane and, with the help of thousands of miles and the distraction of doing good work in the world, to disconnect for a while. I hoped time and distance would give me space to practice letting go of attachments to the past and to living more gently with things unsettled and unsettling.

TRAVELLING TO AFRICA

The month in Africa would be in three parts. The first week would be in Bujumbura, Burundi, facilitating a Pan-African Conference on leadership competency and coaching style. Bujumbura is on the west coast of the country, at the top of the long lake which is unnamed in the map below; it's Lake Tanganyika. After the conference, I would leave Heidrun and the team and fly east to Tanzania for the remaining three weeks: two weeks to climb Mt. Kilimanjaro, which is just next to the Kenyan border, between Arusha and Moshi; and the final week to see the Great Migration on the Serengeti plains.

I flew from Philadelphia to Dulles in D.C., and thought I'd use the USAirways Club to pass the time with free snacks in the lounge. But the pass I had wasn't valid in this club. I calculated the time in Mexico and called Alan to get a club code from him (he travels a lot for business), and they let me in. I did tell him about the day-early arrival at the airport, asked him not to worry, and reminded him that I'd be electronically disconnected soon. I called Verizon to shut down the phone for the month and save money, since it wouldn't work at all outside the U.S.

I left D.C. at noon, flew overnight to Addis Ababa in Ethiopia. For this travel I avoided all alcohol, ate lightly and stayed awake as much as possible. During the flights I had time to prepare for what was ahead: I reviewed the printed notes for the Leadership Conference, mentally rehearsing what I could. When I didn't want to concentrate on anything in particular, I chilled out with a few movies and did some sewing for Kilimanjaro. I sewed strings onto the sides of the SPF hat I borrowed from my Mom and sewed the edges of two green-and-pink-swirled quilt squares that would serve as handkerchiefs, all the while amazed that it was okay to have a sewing needle on an airplane.

I also read and re-read the Security Plan for Burundi that had been provided to all conference participants. I wanted to be intimately familiar with the security protocol, so that I could respond appropriately to any situation that might occur. The plan discussed "likely threats to personal security" based on the historical and current situation there, and provided "advice on appropriate behavior" including what to do in the event of an emergency.

From the report, I learned that Burundi (one of the ten poorest countries in the world) and its neighbors, Rwanda and the Democratic Republic of Congo (DRC) have been through turbulent times since the 1990s, with hundreds of thousands of people being killed during conflicts spanning more than a decade. During this time, hundreds of thousands more became refugees, fleeing from Burundi to Tanzania and from DRC to Burundi. The report also described people-trafficking and child abuse in Burundi, where children were used as soldiers and exploited in domestic and sexual servitude. In 2003, the area got relief from war with the Arusha Peace Accord. Since then, thousands of refugees have returned home.

The report also indicated that in Burundi, especially in its capital, Bujumbura, "the situation was stable." Though peaceful, Bujumbura is, nonetheless, like any other city around the world, a place to remain "aware" and "streetwise." Travel outside areas that are known to be safe was not recommended, since robbery and murder can occur in outlying areas, where there are still social conflicts. I read the risk analysis on robberies, car thefts, ambushes, road blocks, land mines, and small arms/grenades. There were standard operating procedures for all types of emergency and life-threatening situations, including political unrest.

I knew I'd be with professionals, some local, and others from across the continent, all familiar with cultural and safety protocol. I knew that I'd be in good hands, and that I'd be safe. Nonetheless, I realized while reading the security briefing, that a cell phone would have been a good thing to have, just in case. But I didn't have one that would work in Africa.

After a three-hour layover in Ethiopia, I took the next flight to Kigali, Rwanda, where we didn't even leave the plane during the half-hour stop. From Rwanda the plane continued on; it was a short flight to Bujumbura, Burundi, where the local time at landing was 1:30 in the afternoon on June 4th. Don't ask me how long the flight time was. Though I'm sure I could calculate it[3], I've always travelled with the intention to "be where I am"—to sleep when it's dark and wake when it's light. Most of the time it even works.

It was bright and sunny in Burundi and, despite the long journey, I was excited to arrive. I was especially thrilled that all of my luggage made it AND to see the van from the hotel—all good signs that I was certainly off to a most excellent start!

The drive to the hotel (and back to the airport) was the extent of what I'd see of life in Burundi outside the hotel

---

3 I calculated it. 8,391 miles. 25 hours.

complex. Despite being densely populated, according to the report I'd read, I saw only a few cars. Most of the people I saw were walking, some riding bicycles and most carrying huge sacks—bigger than a linebacker—on either the front or back of their bikes, or balanced on their heads. The driver told me the sacks were filled with potatoes; I wondered how heavy those sacks were, and how the bicycle tires handled the weight. The bicycle riders were mostly men.

Women wrapped in brightly patterned African cloth were walking alongside the road confidently; many wore flip-flops and I wondered how many times stones got between their feet and the shoe. Their loads appeared heavy, yet they moved with grace; straight-up, eyes-ahead posture to maintain balance for the large bags and bundles atop their heads.

We drove by an expansive U.N. refugee camp, its high, gray cement walls topped with intimidating coils of heavy barbed wire. The camp lined the road for several blocks. It was quiet; I saw no movement, as though the place was abandoned, yet United Nations statistics indicate that more than 200,000 refugees lived there then. The appearance and feel of the scene reminded me of *District 9*, a gritty film about fear, man's inhumanity to man and the experience of being an outsider in your own land. It was distressing to me, to know that people lived behind these gray, barbed-wire walls. It looked more like a prison than any camp I'd ever known. Understanding that the high security is there to protect those within the walls doesn't make it any more inviting, or any less disturbing.

Often, when I see news reports of refugees around the world, I try to imagine what it would be like to leave behind all that you know as home. I cannot imagine how much courage it would require. My heart hurts when I think about families who've been faced with the decision. How bad does it have to be to decide that the best move you can make is to pack up your children and to leave everything behind? I wonder if I had to do it, would I be able to, or would I optimistically hold on to the hope things would get better?

*   *   *

Arriving at the hotel, we pulled into the well-guarded, walled and gated entrance. I later learned that it serves as a vacation club for ex-patriots and others in the area. The hotel was lovely. My ground-level room was big and clean, with mosquito netting over the bed and a view overlooking the Olympic-sized pool. Surrounding the pool were more than a dozen small tables with chairs; each table was topped by a thatched umbrella to provide shade. I unpacked, washed up, and then headed out to find my companions in this place, which would be my home, for work, for the next week.

I left my room, rounded the corner and found myself staring at a beautiful white sandy beach on what looked like an ocean with medium waves and good wind. It was actually Lake Tanganyika, an African Great Lake, the second largest freshwater lake in the world by volume, and the second deepest after Lake Baikal in Siberia. It is also the world's longest freshwater lake. The water from Lake Tanganyika flows into the Congo River system, and, ultimately, into the Atlantic Ocean. Thanks to our prime location on this magnificent lake, we enjoyed fresh grilled fish each night at dinner, and wonderful breezes as we dined in covered dining rooms that lined the sandy beach.

Security was tight. I was instructed by signs and during our host's security briefing that we were not to go onto the beach before 6 a.m. or after 6 p.m. Uniformed and armed guards, both hotel security and military, provided stealth patrols over all the grounds and were a visible presence along the beach. Walking to my room after dinner one evening, I sensed someone else was near and realized there was a darkly-dressed armed guard in the garden just beyond my room. Rebel fighting is a long-standing situation in the mountain areas 40 kilometers beyond town and travel in that area is not recommended. For me, I never left the compound during my stay. My days were busy and full, and I used any down time to mentally recharge for the activities of my work there.

There were opportunities to exercise in Burundi. There was that Olympic swimming pool, a small open-air gym, and a beautiful beach. I visited the gym a couple of times and walked on the beach, though never alone. Beach walking was best in small groups or pairs. One of my favorite walks was with Karimi, an impressive woman from the conference who had accomplished so much in her professional life, while at the same time raising a young family. I appreciated the opportunity to get to know her.

I can't remember now if I brought a bathing suit with me. Nonetheless, weighing in at a record number, I didn't feel much like swimming, although several people from the group could be seen taking laps at all times of the day.

In the pool area I was very pleased to recognize someone I knew. Rebecca was the only person attending the conference whom I'd actually met face-to-face before. Rebecca is now my African partner in Coaches Without Borders; together, she and I led the activities of the successful pilot program in Ghana. We had met a couple of months ago when she spoke at a conference near my home. She's another smart, accomplished woman, a fellow lifelong learner (she's in law school as I'm writing this) and mother of two. It was comforting and so nice to see a familiar face. We chatted about our respective journeys getting there and about the hotel itself, both agreeing it was a very nice place for the conference.

Rebecca let me borrow a conference team computer to check email back home. I had determined to travel lightly on this trip, especially on Kilimanjaro, which included a complete disconnect—no computer, no Internet, no telephone. I made sure to communicate this intention to all of my clients, friends, family and contacts over the weeks before leaving, so all bases were covered at home. I didn't dare reply to any of the new emails in order to maintain the boundary: I did not want to negate the good foundation made when I left. I did, however, sneak in two important emails (typos thanks to my lack of familiarity with a non-U.S. keyboard):

> [From Email] *Email #1—6/4 Deb to Alan: Hi honey, have arrived in /burundi and it's lovely. warm and breezy, sitting by the pool now having unpacked and showered—how nice that was! \borrowing a computer from \tanya who is coordinating the conference. we are 6 hours ahead of you there. just arranged for a phone which i will have by tomorrow or monday. hope you enjoyed a great siteseeing and cultural day; i'm about to be immersed in it here. i'm staying in hotel du lac tanganyika . . . quite nice . . . look it up*
>
> *Alan replied "So good to get this email!!!!! Yes I miss you. I will check your website. Have a great time with your workshop. STAY SAFE!!! And enjoy!"*
>
> *Email #2—From Deb to Karen, Linda D on 6/4/2011 quick note to say im here. getting a phone—it's a good idea to have one regardless. it's gorgeous—warm and breezy, the lake looks like the ocean and the pool is inviting. ciao for now.*

I learned from Rebecca that cell phones are relatively inexpensive in Africa, and that the conference arrangers could help me get a phone and SIM card. Remembering the security briefings, I put those wheels in motion.

After enjoying time with Rebecca and being able to use the computer, I finally got to meet Heidrun, whose voice I recognized immediately.

Me and Heidrun

She didn't look at all like I'd expected. Though I hadn't given it too much thought, I assumed she'd look more like me, average height and sturdy build. But Heidrun is quite the opposite; she has a dancer's body—tall and thin. I wasn't surprised to see bright eyes and a big smile, but was surprised by the delightful dimples that came with it, along with lovely skin and soft, brown, pinned up curls. She was wearing a stunning outfit, one of the long skirt-and-top ensembles that I'd heard about, made for her in Ghana. She'd worked with a dressmaker in Ghana who selected the fabrics, designed the pieces and hand-made whole outfits for Heidrun. I will confess to you that I had a very clear thought: wishing we were closer to Ghana so I might meet this dressmaker.

It was so nice to finally give and receive a hug from this dear friend. We chatted for a short time but this group of three action-oriented women didn't stay still for long; we had to get busy.

We got to work checking out the space and setting up, planning for the days ahead, when about 40 people, leaders of aid activity in-country from 13 countries across Africa, and some from the

U.K. home office, would gather for self- and program-development, knowledge- and skill-building, and information-sharing. They'd come to learn with and from each other.

As the days proceeded, I learned more about the amazing people who came together here, about their work and way of living, their commitment to the work they do, and to the people whose lives they touch. Their humanitarian work includes disaster response, advocacy, risk reduction and resiliency. They see some of the harshest situations of mankind, and injustices they work hard to eliminate, with few resources. Their motto is pOVERty—poverty over—and in my experience, it is quite clear that each one is committed to the practicality of such a vision.

Their programs are targeted to right injustices that in so many spheres would be overwhelming to most of us even to comprehend, yet they do it with commitment, intelligence and grace. I appreciated the glimpse into their work and lives. Over the week, I learned about some of the people themselves in session, at break, during meals, sitting by the pool, and walking on the beach. The conversations were powerful, insightful, and certain ones of them will undoubtedly stay with me for a very long time.

My original "charter" with Heidrun was to co-lead a full-day Coaching Atelier. "What is an "atelier," you ask?" I did too, and Heidrun told me it's French for "workshop." Since I'd probably be there for a couple of days, Heidrun declared that I may as well help with the Leadership part of the conference too. I was thrilled to participate, since this is my work and what I love to do.

In the months leading up to the conference, I was energized discussing Heidrun's vision and brainstorming ideas together. I was happy to be invited to join the planning committee, which involved meeting via Skype on conference calls every few weeks with Heidrun and some of her colleagues in the U.K. and Africa.

The committee created an interactive, experiential two days of activity focused on eight facets of leadership. The structure for the days was established, along with a pattern for consistent delivery. I offered materials and ideas from workshops I'd co-created and delivered on Emotional Intelligence, the Neuroscience of Innovation and Creativity, Coaching and Mindfulness. The presenters would include every member of the committee plus volunteers from the organization who'd already done exemplary work in some of these areas.

We were confident it would be a fun experience for all. We prepared handouts of instruction, explanation, and summaries, so that all the leaders could take back the tools they found most relevant to their own work, to their own country. The first few days included time for each person to evaluate what those take-back items would be for them.

Heidrun and I created the full-day Coaching Atelier using a combination of techniques from her Gestalt work, our work together at the International Coach Academy, and my work at the University of Pennsylvania, where I earned a Master's degree in Organizational Dynamics, as well as graduate certificates in Organizational Coaching, Leadership, and Change Management. The day was full; we employed the "Tell-Show-Do" method (the same we'd used during the first two days) with emphasis on "do." Participants spent most of the time in the Coaching Atelier doing actual coaching, experiencing the challenges and power of it, both as coach and as client. They, and we, also observed others "in action."

The third day included a wrap-up, allowing all participants to reflect and share from their own experience of the first three days, before moving on to subsequent days of sharing best practices and strategic planning.

*　　*　　*

The fourth day finally allowed an opportunity for me to reward myself with a rare bit of shopping. Others from the group in Burundi had gone out to the marketplace earlier in the week but

I'd missed the opportunity, choosing workshop prep instead—out of necessity. The hotel had a small gift shop that I'd passed several times each day, but it was either closed or I was briskly on task. Passing the shop on that fourth day, I saw that it was open, and I had a chance to browse the rack and shelves.

To me, shopping can be as enjoyable as a good meal, and when I travel, I look for mementos to bring home to remind me of that place. Sometimes I find them in a store; other times in more unusual places. I have a horseshoe from Patagonia, thrown by a horse I rode across streams, up hills and on wide open plains. I have two big, bleached-white conch shells with shiny pink interiors that I plucked from white sands under-water in the British Virgin Islands. They sit just outside my office in a blueware soup tureen that was a gift from my sister-in-law, Lynn. I brought home a handmade Bedouin dress, the only one of its kind, from within the walled city of Jerusalem; steak knives from a shop that also sold medieval-looking swords and armor in Toledo, Spain; and chunky glass knife-rests from a junque shop in Paris.

Every time I wear that Bedouin dress, I remember the hospitality of the shop owner, and the impact that being in Jerusalem had on my world view. In that old walled city, four major monotheistic religions live together in close proximity and in peace—something that reminds me about hope—like this conference did.

Whenever I select the hearty, rugged knives from Toledo for dinner, I think of medieval Spain and knights in shining armor; these are knives for big steaks, not dainty fish. I remember when I bought them; it was during my first trip to Spain. I went with three girlfriends. We flew to Spain not long after terrorists bombed the World Trade Center in New York City on September 11th; it was a time when many people were afraid to fly. But we set off with determination, agreeing that we would not let terrorists dictate our travel, or the way we live our lives.

Holding those chunky, old, French glass knife rests in my hand reminds me of wandering through back streets in Paris and window shopping there. Then, I remember picnics with Alan, cobbled together with treats procured from small French shops and outdoor stands: bread, fruit, raw cheeses and wine.

Memories are the opportunity to return to places I've enjoyed. What would I bring home from Burundi?

I found a stylish shirt for Alan, zebra batik in a deep blue, and several choices for me (Jackpot!). Standing behind a ramshackle curtain and swatting at mosquitoes, I tried on a dozen dresses, but I couldn't decide. The saleswoman was lovely and patient, offering her opinions as I asked for them. Narrowing it down to three or four, I still couldn't decide and asked if I could corral some girlfriends to help. She insisted that I take the "finalists" to my room and bring the rest back later, which I did.

It's at times like these that I wish for my sister's perspective. Karen has good taste, knows what looks good on me and isn't afraid to tell me what doesn't, usually with good humor. Fortunately for me, Jeanne Kamara, one of the sweetest women I worked with on the planning committee, agreed to stand in for my sister and help me decide. One by one I tried on the dresses for Jeanne's opinion. Each was hand-dyed, locally-made and uniquely beautiful. One by one they were determined to be too big, too dark, until finally, Jeanne said she thought the gold one with the Egyptian-looking neck-work was just right.

The saleswoman was also pleased with the choice and gave me the gift of a matching beaded necklace. I wore my new ensemble proudly on my final afternoon and evening in Burundi.

*   *   *

At the end of each conference day I reflected on the experience. Feedback from the participants indicated it was powerful and interesting, sometimes fun and sometimes uncomfortable—just what a facilitator would expect from a group that's trying out new behaviors. For example, this workshop included using coaching technique—asking questions and listening deeply rather than giving advice—which is incredibly difficult for leaders used to doing all of the talking, and who often are expected, or required, to be directive, and to be the one to provide the right answer. Some elements of the workshop, like the use of Laughter Yoga[4] to promote innovation and creativity, were met with a full spectrum of reaction: from strong resistance by those who couldn't see the relevance, to cautious excitement by others who thought they might be willing and able to give it a try.

For me, it was work to be there, even though it was as a volunteer and even though I love facilitation. Being "on" all day and evening takes energy. The same thing happens to me after multi-day workshops at home; they're fun but they're work, and I need to recharge when I'm through. I spent quiet time in my room to recharge in Burundi each day, and read an inspirational piece I brought along called, *A Prayer for Inner Peace*[5]:

> May today there be peace within.
>
> May you trust that you are exactly where you are meant to be.
>
> May you not forget the infinite possibilities that are born of faith in yourself and others.
>
> May you use the gifts that you have received, and pass on the love that has been given to you.
>
> May you be content with yourself just the way you are.

---

[4] Laughter Yoga, developed by Dr. Madan Kataria, is based on scientific evidence of physiological and psychological benefits from unconditional laughter. It's fun and feels like play, which makes it appear less serious than it actually is. I've found it to be an excellent exercise for stimulating the brain and the heart, as well as the ideas that come from the combination of the two.

[5] I love this poem and have it framed in my office, next to my desk. I didn't realize who wrote it until I thought to include it in this book and looked it up; it's attributed to Mother Teresa of Calcutta. It has been a favorite of mine ever since January 3, 2008, when I received it as a wish for the New Year from my friend Rebecca Kingsley.

Let this knowledge settle into your bones, and allow your soul the freedom to sing, dance, praise and love.

It is there for each and every one of us.

On my last night in Burundi, I called my mom on the cell phone that Andre, our in-country host, had procured for me. I described the beautiful moon over the water, the beach and the peaceful scene around the pool. After the call ended I cried, feeling worn out from the work and missing home. Had the time difference finally set in? I don't think so.

*   *   *

Before I left on this African adventure, my friend, Mike Dougherty, handed me the current day's page from his Dalai Lama calendar, *Insights* from Friday, May 27, 2011. I carried that piece of paper with me across Africa, in my notebook, as a reminder. I offered the quote in an email of thanks, after my return, to the folks I worked with in Burundi.

> "People merely involved in their own progress, lack the magnificence of those who are willing to dwell in the blazing fire of the pains of the world, in order to remove even one type of suffering from a single sentient being."

I received emails months after the work in Burundi, some from people who'd been skeptical about the in-session work. One brave woman challenged herself to do Laughter Yoga with her team, something completely outside the box for her and for them. I was thrilled to hear about her bravery and the success she had with it. Another emailed to ask for more information on the neuroscience behind innovation and creativity, to share with her team. It's rewarding to know that the work is being carried forward by these impressive leaders.

Day 1

[From notebook]   *Reflections en route to JRO (Kilimanjaro Airport):*

Sad to be leaving but ready. At the Burundi airport they are expecting me because my flight was changed and left two days ago. But no worries, they find a solution eventually. Thank goodness we left early from the hotel. I have a strange sense of foreboding when they wish me "bonne chance" as I walk across the tarmac to board the small plane.

Arrive Kigali, Rwanda. My flight left a few minutes ago. Seems they just decided to change the departure time from 14:55 to 12:15. C'est la vie. Just sit here and be patient please, and no need to worry about your passport, that man you had to give it to is from immigration and he'll give it back to you when you have a boarding pass.

I wanted information, details. I could feel myself slipping into high-stress, high-strung "pushy Deb" mode.

The most possible way to JRO it seems, is via Nairobi. The next flight there is 6 hours from now. Thank goodness too, because it takes more than four hours to locate my luggage (excitement, relief, it is here!) and make arrangements for the tickets. There is much to discuss and debate between Kenya Air and Rwandair and it takes time.

Everything, it seems, takes time. Dinner in Burundi took an hour to be served most nights, since everything is fresh and prepared to order. It took literally, just shy of two hours to be served one night when the whole group was seated at once!

I was reminded of the importance of breathing deeply to relax. I gave it a try. Eventually it kicked in and my nerves calmed, my expression relaxed; my energy became patient and open. I widened my shoulders to open my heart and repeated the mantra, "Please let them find what they need to give me what I need."

Jullius Mutia, Station Manager at Kigali for Kenya Airways, assures me that "everything works for good." And you know what? About two hours into this, my patience wrapped around me, I am in the flow and resigned to let all things happen for good, and THIS is when solutions are finalized. Now, there are more smiles all around.

At one point, Julius told me it would cost another US$150 for the new ticket; he asked if I had the cash. "Yes," I told him, "just let me go to the bathroom and then I'll get it for you." Everything is done in cash on a trip like this and I had a few thousand dollars in large and small bills on my person. Literally. I had $3,000 stored in snack-size zip-lock bags (the perfect size for U.S. currency). The bags were each wrapped in lovely fabric to help with perspiration, since those pretty packets were lining my bra cups, one on each side, for balance, of course.

But wait, there is more, and it's the best part (maybe my cosmic reward for patience?). Julius later learned that my original class of ticket meant I didn't have to pay the extra fee. Now, I would have no way of knowing any of this, and I was okay giving them another $150 if I could just get to Kilimanjaro and not have to spend the night in the Kigali airport. But he told me this was the case and returned the $150 to me.

In a part of the world where corruption is expected (not unlike some places in the U.S., I should point out), he could easily have kept the money, but didn't. Sometimes we meet angels along our way and I believe Julius is one of them.

At this point, the folks from SENE in Kilimanjaro were about to leave for the two-hour drive to the airport to pick me up. But with this new flight I wouldn't be there at 5:00 p.m. as originally planned. I'd be there at 11:00 p.m., assuming all went well. Anxious, I wanted to call them so they wouldn't drive all the way out and have to sit in the airport for six hours. But my inexpensive mobile phone from Burundi didn't work in Rwanda, and Kigali is a small airport in which, especially on a Sunday, I couldn't buy a phone card. I described the situation to Julius and he made the call for me, catching the driver just in time—he'd just left, but they were able to call him back before he got too far up the road.

"All things happen for good."

–Julius M. Mutia, Station Manager for Kenya Airways in Kigali International Airport, Rwanda.

[From Notebook] *The flight arrangements made, I checked my bags and met more drama. "You have two bags?" she asked, "Yes," I answered, "I'll be in Africa for a month." I sensed this was leading to something more, specifically to the possibility that I would have to pay more for the weight of the bags, or for one or both of them. I made the smart decision to leave the situation in the hands of the very capable professionals, silently repeating my mantra with an open heart and calm demeanor. She tagged both bags and pushed them back for loading onto the plane. I thanked her for her help today.*

This young woman, who has seen me here all afternoon (it's a small airport), asked in a voice edged with pleading, "Why don't you stay here for a while, visit in Rwanda?" It's hard to say no to someone so sincere.

I explained that my itinerary was set, that reservations were made and that I was obligated to others for this trip, but that I'd heard how beautiful her country is and hoped that I might visit another time.

The conversation left a lasting impression.

During the exchange with the bag checker I recalled a story I'd heard the previous week from Helen, one of the people I met in Burundi who impressed me the most. Helen has an amazing background including diplomatic roles and non-governmental organization (NGO) work. She is a person who knows how to handle adversity, facing it head on, and has done so, many times over her life and career.

Helen told me a story about her work in Africa, near the end of the genocide in Rwanda, when they'd lost contact with a female aide worker inside the country. No one from the office was willing to go into the war-torn country to find and rescue their colleague. So Helen drove in, found the woman, and got her out safely.

She talked about the dangers of the ride in a succinct way that a story is sometimes told, and I cannot imagine what it was like, or how it felt to be in the middle of such a dangerous situation, with so many unknowns. Helen, I should mention to you, was probably under 40 years old at the time of this rescue and is a petite, pale-skinned Caucasian woman with red hair—not someone who would blend in easily in Rwanda.

The story continues when, almost a decade later, Helen found herself back in Rwanda, driving through what she described as "beautiful rolling hills." She said she felt almost guilty to be enjoying the beauty she saw around her on this drive, because she remembered what it was like not even ten years before. Helen is brave; she is a modern day Athena. I hope someday she'll write her story, since what I know of it has inspired me and I'd love to know more. I know she'd inspire others.

I may not be able to return to Rwanda today, but I feel a connection. I had a choice of buying coffee from Colombia or Rwanda the other day and chose . . . Rwandan.

Waiting for my flight, I was enjoying Aljazeera TV in the Kigali airport lounge, munching on some granola I brought with me and a bottle of sparkling water from the café. It was almost time for the short flight to Nairobi. I was ready.

Nairobi is a big city[6]. The airport is much bigger than Rwanda's and has an international look and feel. I saw planes on the tarmac

---

[6] According to the CIA Fact Sheet, Kenya's capital city of Nairobi is the largest city in East Africa, despite being the youngest city in the region, with a population estimated to exceed three million people. Rwanda's capital, Kigali, by comparison, is less than one-third the size; it has about 750,000 people.

from Emirates, KLM and more. Inside the terminal it was commercial, with a tempting line of shops along one full side of the long, wrap-around hallway. I was sure there were bargains to be found there, but it was not to be for me because I was a woman on a mission. I'd learned from my seatmate on the last flight that the best place to procure a phone card was from a small kiosk at the end of the international terminal. I speed-walked my way through the crowd to get there, passing the shiny shops and all their wares with nothing but quick looks as I walked by. A brisk walk and US$40 later, I had a new SIM card which, the salesman assured me, would definitely work in Tanzania.

*   *   *

I arrived at JRO at 11:00 p.m. The airport security/customs officer was testy—I guess I might be too at 11:00 p.m. with a bunch of tired tourists descending on my airport—but that didn't bother me. I was so relieved to see my driver that it didn't matter.

I was greeted by Joseph Matula, my driver from SENE. We collected my bags, walked out into the cool night and found the car, a rugged jungle-green Land Rover. I settled in for the two-hour ride to Simon's farm, wide awake thanks to the fresh evening air and the buzz of curiosity that being in a new place brings. The ride out of the airport was smooth.

Driving along the dark highways, on the "British side" of the road, I asked Joseph about his habit of putting on the right blinker when a car passed on the right side, the driver's side. He told me it's common practice and done to establish boundaries, to alert the oncoming driver who may or may not be so alert, to the dimensions of the vehicle. That made sense to me, and I was glad to be with a competent driver.

We slowed down when driving through little towns and a good thing too, as there were a lot of people and dogs roaming the roads, especially around the small, well-lit bars along the way.

At one point we were pulled over by a policewoman and I wasn't sure what to do. In his book, Stedman advised that if this happens, don't say a thing and let the guide handle everything since often it's simply a matter of paying the bribe for passage; the driver will know what to do. I recalled instantly the articles from Alan about tourists being kidnapped, and was fearful of making eye contact with the woman, even when she asked me a question. Instead I looked at Joseph and asked, "What should I do?" He told me it was okay to answer her. "I'm here to climb Kilimanjaro with Simon Mtuy's company, SENE. I just came in from Burundi to the airport." Then, to my great relief, she waved us on. We were allowed to pass without incident and I remembered what Julius said, that "all things happen for good."

I learned from Joseph that this too is a standard practice, to stop cars along the road. He told me that he actually knew the woman from school. I would learn later, from another driver, that it's less common for a climbing or safari vehicle to be pulled over, especially when there is clearly a client or clients inside. He told me that tourism is a commonly respected thing, acknowledged by most in Tanzania as important for the local economy, and on-road harassment would clearly have an adverse impact on tourism dollars coming to the region.

Still, it's not uncommon for company drivers to learn via briefings and phone calls where these pull-overs are likely to be so they can avoid them, if possible. I suggested they create life-sized cardboard cutouts of tourist-looking people to sit up in the seats of the Land Rover.

Riding past small towns marked by no more than a dozen shacks in connected clusters along the road, and two bigger towns (which I later learned were Moshi and Arusha), we eventually came to an area that felt more rural, and broke off the paved road. We rode in over a rugged stretch of washed-out, rocky road, and as we climbed to 6,000 feet, the air was noticeably cooler.

Porters greeted us at the top of the road and took the luggage out of the car. In the distance I could see the lights of the farm, which was lit up like a beacon for us. I hopped out of the car, pulled the straps of my backpack on, and adjusted my headlamp, which I'd had at the ready. I remembered from my "last minute details" packet, that SENE had suggested that guests arriving at night would need their headlamps to get to the farm.

The porters were already taking the luggage out of the back and one lifted my large hard-sided suitcase right up and onto his head in one swift motion. My first instinct was that I shouldn't allow him to do that, but then I reminded myself: this is how it's done. I and my backpack followed the porters, who were carrying my body-sized duffel bag and suitcase on their heads, along a dirt path lined by low, big palm leaves and past a stream that I could hear but could not see. Our headlamps lit the way for our feet as we made our way up the uneven and slick dirt path to the farm.

The lights were brighter as we got closer to Mbahe Farm and I was greeted warmly by a whole team, including Benard, who was something like my Butler. I also met Pascal, who seemed to run the place, and "Sugar Ray" Leonard, my chef. Pascal told me that Leonard's name did not actually include "Sugar Ray," but Pascal added it so that I would remember his name is Leonard.

Leonard handed me a plate of huge, warm cashews, fresh from the local farm, blackened and just roasted, along with a glass of cold, thick, fresh tropical fruit juice. We sat by the roaring fire in oversized cushioned chairs in a partially open, partially tented area next to the house. It was 1:00 a.m. and I was tired, but grateful for the delicious snack, warm fire and hearty greeting.

I learned that they'd turned the generators on just for my arrival and that they'd keep them on as long as I liked. I asked for half an hour and remained by the fire for another few minutes, then went in to my room, which was directly off the stone deck of the patio we were sitting on. It was time to wash up and hit the sack.

[From my notebook] *Welcome to Mbahe Village, located in the foothills of Mt. Kilimanjaro, welcome to Tanzania. May you sleep well.*

DAY 2

[From my SENE itinerary] *Mbahe Village Farm Cottages (6,000'). "You have the morning to rest and relax. Enjoy delicious "homebrew" coffee, grown and roasted on the farm, and meals made with fruits and vegetables from the garden. Your trip leader will provide a climb orientation and equipment check. This is also a day to take a guided tour around Mbahe Village, the Mtuy family farm, and to swim in the river and waterfall running through Simon's land."*

Awakened by the sounds of people milling around outside my room on the "house" side, I got out of bed and threw on some clothes, sleepy but eager to look around in the daylight. I found a landscape that was lush, even in winter time. A small pasture, complete with cows, was just beyond the wooden gate. Tended gardens were all around the property which included a main house, the large guest cottage that I stayed in, the substantially-tented dining and sitting area I enjoyed last evening, and three newly-constructed, connecting guest cottages below, directly adjacent to the vegetable garden.

Morning sun danced on the colors—every shade of green, some yellow and a red flowering plant that caught my eye because there, dipping into the small red flowers, was an iridescent blue-green bird.

Reading through Stedman's guide before I'd left home, I found color photos of birds, monkeys, rodents, lizards and plants that one could expect to see on Kilimanjaro. Of them all, there was one bird in particular—the Malachite Sunbird—that I'd hoped to see. Breathtakingly bright green and blue, it looked like a jewel in the photo, just stunning. Before I left home I'd thought to myself, wouldn't it be wonderful to see that bird?

It was smaller than I'd expected, based on the photo, and fast. I learned later that the birds at Mbahe Farm are Variable Sunbirds, which are similar in coloring to the Malachite Sunbird but smaller, and bright-yellow breasted. It was a beautiful thing to see in the morning sunlight and in that moment, it seemed to me

48

that a wish I'd made had been granted. I was excited by this little gift and filled with gratitude; I had a sense that it was there to welcome me to Tanzania, to Kilimanjaro.

Mbahe Farm is actually on Mt. Kilimanjaro, across but some distance from the Machame gate which leads to the Machame trail, one of the trekking routes for Mt. Kilimanjaro. I looked often for this little bird while I stayed on the farm and enjoyed watching it flit around the red-flowering plant it liked so much. I took a few videos to bring home and share with Mom, who loves birds and loves to bird watch. What a gift!

I had breakfast with Pascal, who I learned later is the brother-in-law of one of my guides, Wilson. Pascal greeted me and said, "You are like Jane Goodall," which struck me as funny; I was both complimented, as he intended, and proud of myself. "Yes," I realized, "I am a woman travelling through East Africa solo. And I'm about to climb Mt. Kilimanjaro solo, too." Well, sort of . . . there would be a team to support me.

Breakfast was hearty and started with platters of fruits, all local, all organic, all delicious. The juice was thick, rich, blended tropical nectar. The coffee was light, and I decided that my second cup would be Earl Grey tea. The honey knocked my socks off! Also organic and from Mbahe Farm, I found out that the honey is from killer bees and the hive was here on the farm, just off the path we traversed last night.

After breakfast I met Honest Matto, my guide, when he joined us for a planning meeting. We reviewed the maps and the plan, and I signed some kind of waiver—*hakuna matata* (Swahili for no problems/no worries).

Following the debrief I told Honest about places I was looking forward to that we hadn't discussed yet in the itinerary: to see the ash pit when we were up in the crater, and I asked if it was possible to get to the place where the ground is warm to the touch. "Yes, it is possible, and we will try to do this," Honest said. I later learned that it's important to make these agreements up front, before you climb, since last minute changes in the plan sometimes result in extra charges, which is fair.

I laid out all of my clothing and equipment on the bed for inspection, leaving the business clothes from the first week in the suitcase, along with some of the clothes I wanted to keep clean for safari the final week. I was careful to take only what I was certain to need on the mountain since somebody would have to carry it. Pascal and Honest quickly surveyed the items and made a few suggestions. They advised me to bring one of the two down coats that I'd brought along and planned to give away at the end of the climb. The coat would be easy to bring along since it's light and easily compressed in the giant zip-lock bags that I'd been using, which they thought were an exceptional idea (virtual pat on the back for that!)

The bags were the type that you suck the air out of with a vacuum cleaner, and they worked exceptionally well for this packing because I could crush down the bag by lying on top of it to expel the air from the contents, and then zip it up for compact bundles and easier storage, easier packing.

My clothing and equipment were approved, and then it was time for a walk around the farm. We walked up, down and around and I think this gave them a chance to see how I might perform on the climb. On the way, Pascal entertained us with stories of other guests who'd been there.

[From my notebook] *Reflections on the stories of Otto and Martin.*

Otto attempted the summit three times; it took him over a month, but he kept trying until he succeeded. Motto: You may not make it, but don't give up.

Martin was a heavy smoker and came to the farm with a lot of coughing. The clean air here from so many trees was good for his lungs and in three days his lungs cleared and the cough dissipated. Motto: This place is good for you!

I heard these stories on our walk through the other Wachagga (also known as Chagga) farms in Mbahe village. I saw coffee, bananas, sweet potatoes, flowers, palms, pines, eucalyptus and waterfalls plucked straight out of paradise. There were cows and goats and a gaggle of kids playing in the stream far below "Jambo, jambo—come down and play with us!"[7]

In a short time we were on our way back, and we were gingerly approached by the gaggle of tots, who ranged from maybe three to five years old. They were sweet and friendly, with runny noses and big smiles and they wanted to hold my hand and practice their English. We made a circle and danced around while they said, "Hello madam, how are you?" and "thank you," smiling and giggling in between. Smiles and giggles and innocent eyes staring up—except two little ones, who I suspect were afraid of me because they didn't join in, they just stood there and cried. The kids followed us for a while, and I wished I'd thought to bring treats for them.

I saw women with huge bags of fodder (grasses to feed animals) or six foot long bundles of wood; they carried them on their heads. Honest insisted on holding my water bottle and I held the camera. Pascal showed me the border to Kenya—it's so close.

*   *   *

At dinner that evening on Mbahe Farm, I was joined by four teachers who were staying in the guest cottages next to the vegetable garden. They'd been teaching at the Mwenge University College of Education in Moshi for a while, but recently the funding ended and it was almost time for them to leave. They appeared to be two couples, Karl and Edit, the more senior, and Anna and Simon, the younger couple. They'd come

---

[7] Jambo is the Swahili word for "hello."

51

to Simon's for a getaway weekend in the cool, quiet, clean mountains, and to enjoy beautiful day hikes. Karl had been scavenging the wooded area that day for medicinal herbs. They shared their South African wine with me, which I both appreciated and enjoyed; it was a pleasant surprise to have good wine.

I hadn't had any wine since leaving the states, not even on the plane. In fact, I suspect my easy adjustment to the time zone of Africa (+7 hours from the U.S.) was partly due to the fact that I didn't drink any alcohol during the flights, and I stayed awake as long as I possibly could. But on this night, I allowed myself to enjoy a glass of wine with dinner, compliments of my dining companions.

*   *   *

I was eager to try out my new phone card, the one that would most certainly work in Tanzania. Phoning home proved to be quite difficult on this trip, however, for several reasons.

While I was in Burundi, Alan was in Asia, a straight 12-hour time difference. I did manage to reach him by phone twice from Burundi, but calls from Tanzania would prove to be more challenging, even with the SIM card that was "certain" to work here. Stedman advises that if your call doesn't go through dialing regularly, it may work by dialing an extra zero before the number. I tried it. That didn't work for me. I played with the sequence and discovered that with two extra zeros, it did work. Sometimes. Thankfully it worked enough for me to connect with Alan once before leaving Mbahe Farm, to let him know I'd arrived in Tanzania safely. Telecommunications is, as Stedman advises, "hit or miss" on Kilimanjaro.

DAY 3

[From my SENE itinerary] *Simba Farm (5,800').* *"In the morning we depart on the 3-hour drive to Simba Farm in West Kilimanjaro. Simba is an old colonial farm presently owned by the Bruinsma family, good friends of Simon who have farmed in Tanzania for over 25 years. The farm produces market vegetables and barley and wheat for local beer companies. The setting offers breathtaking views of the African savanna and Mount Meru to the west. Above the farm is the lush mountain forest, where we will hike for 2 to 3 hours to a gorge where Colobus monkeys can be seen. We all gather together for dinner to discuss final details and anticipate the start of the climb tomorrow. "*

Before we left Mbahe, I packed just what I needed for the mountain in my backpack and duffel. I put the rest of the items in my suitcase and then locked it with a small combination lock. I gave the locked suitcase to one of the staff for safekeeping until I returned for it in ten days, after my successful summit of Mt. Kilimanjaro, of course.

Joseph arrived and I followed him along the path to the Land Rover waiting below. We stopped after a few minutes to collect Honest, who lives near Simon. The three of us drove out, in the direction of the airport, through Arusha, and then in another direction to get to the SENE office.

Along the way, we passed stands offering fresh, local fruits and vegetables for sale and I asked Joseph (who I learned is actually called Josefu), if it was possible to get some of those tree tomatoes I enjoyed in Burundi—they were small and sweet, like passion fruit + tomato, but dark red or black. "Yes, the

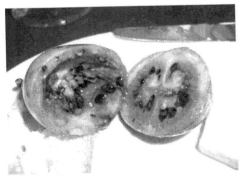

Tamarillo, a.k.a. Tree Tomato

chef has received the request," he assured me.

We drove to the SENE office where I met Paul, a SENE manager from Kenya, and I gave him most of my money (reserving a small amount of currency just in case I needed it) and my passport, to keep in the safe. It was a move of faith, like leaving my luggage behind at Mbahe Farm, or giving my passport to the immigration official at Kigali airport, but I did it because it seemed the only choice. As we were driving away, I remembered that I had forgotten to count it, but I knew it was roughly $2,700 in cash that I'd previously been carrying around in my bra. I remembered too that, "all things happen for good."

Josefu, Honest and I drove out to Simba Farm where we were to stay for the night. Simba Farm is close to the Lemosho gate of Kilimanjaro National Park, our destination for the next day. It also happens to be where Simon was married, so it's a SENE favorite and I can see why.

Simba Farm is a large, commercial farm owned by a Dutch couple and run by the husband's brother. We met our host, his nephew and a friend of theirs from a nearby farm; the three men were enjoying a beer at the end of the work day and would be joining us for dinner.

We left the bags in the room, and sat around in chairs out back, in the shade on a warm, sunny day, while we waited for the previous guests to clear out.

There was a strange vibe going on that I couldn't quite figure out. I sensed alert cautiousness from Josefu and Honest. There seemed to be some sort of friction between them and our host, but I couldn't get a handle on just what it was. Something about the feel of it reminded me of South Africa and apartheid. Was it the Dutch accent? I wasn't sure then, and am still not sure. Whatever it was, it remained palpable into the evening.

Once we'd settled in, the warmth of the day began to subside. It was winter here and not hot. The sun, that had been high and bright during the day, now began to set, and although it was still only late afternoon, in a few hours, it would be an early winter evening in Africa.

Josefu and Honest announced that it was time to explore the area in this beautiful light, so we headed out for a walking adventure. We walked down the long dirt driveway lined at first by beautiful, huge flowering plants and trees. Then the landscape opened up to tawny, farmed fields on both sides.

We got lost leaving the farm through a "shortcut" that one of the guys, either Josefu or Honest, knew about. We walked through high grasses and ended up covered in burrs from chest to toe. We stopped for several minutes to pick the burrs off ourselves and each other. Along the way we met resplendent and regal roosters who were lording over their lands. And we greeted their human owners with a *jambo*!

After the slight detour on the shortcut, we turned left onto the same red-dirt road that we'd come in on earlier in the day. Bikes, cars and trucks passed us, and people hopped on and off at a local stop that appeared to be, based on the twenty-some people there, a local hangout as well. Josefu and Honest asked the locals if they knew the whereabouts of the trailhead we were looking for. Following their directions, we walked down the road just a few yards more, crossed to the other side, stepped over tall grasses and into the woods.

The air was fragrant with scents of fall grass and earth, and the sun hadn't sunk too low yet; it was a well-chosen time of day for this walk. The itinerary says it's a two to three hour hike, but time has a different sensation in Africa and I think I could have walked all day without realizing how many hours had passed. Mother Nature certainly knows how to keep a person entertained with the peaceful wonders of this place.

Making our way through the woods we came across a makeshift camp where one lone guardian lived out a rustic existence. His job was to watch over the water, which I learned is pumped through and filtered at this spot, before being delivered to the local area. I learned too, at dinner later that evening, that there are some tricky regulations for use of this important resource by a large, white-owned farm, even though the Bruinsmas had been there at Simba Farm for more than 25 years. The caretaker wasn't in residence when we passed through.

We kept walking up, down and around a path through the lush forest. The trees grew several stories high and up a steep incline ahead of us. Josefu told me a very sad story about an elephant. Lost, hungry and wandering through the higher part of this area in the dark of night, it fell over a cliff and landed on the jungle floor below.

Climbing up a small incline, we reached a dense spot where the guides stopped and pointed . . . to our left, jumping through the

branches of the tall trees, we saw a family of Colobus monkeys.

Colobus monkeys[8] have long, fluffy white tails, the length of which is about equal to their height of roughly 18-24 inches. They have small, slender black bodies with long-haired white fur down either side, and their faces—black eyes, nose and mouth—are ringed with white fur; their skull, like most of their body, is covered in the same black fur.

Can you imagine what this little monkey looks like as he, or she, flies through the trees from

---

[8] Photo by fellow Kili climber, Stig Nygaard.
www.flickr.com/photos/stignygaard/2226203329/. Used with permission.

branch to branch? I have some video, but the monkeys are tough to see because they move quickly. To me, they were like jungle ninjas, stealth and sure in their leaps, their long tails flying behind them like the streamers on a little girl's bike handles.

They reminded me of a dream I have some times. In this dream I am a female Ninja Warrior from the movie, *Crouching Tiger, Hidden Dragon* and I am running on bamboo . . . seriously, I have this dream. Standing there, watching those monkeys leaping through the trees, I thought of what it must feel like to fly, and I remembered the feeling of that dream.

I stood there in the dense forest, definitely off-trail if there ever was a trail back here, wondering if it was a good idea to be standing there. I had a quick but passing sense of jungle insects crawling around and for just a second I thought, "Maybe I should be moving out of the brush." But the alarm went unheeded as Josefu pointed to something I must see. He pointed out a Mama, "See her there? Her baby is clinging tightly just beneath her chin," and I watched her with interest as she made her way from one branch to the next, in quick succession, all the time with her baby clinging to her chest. I was, once again, overwhelmed with gratitude for the experience. Being there in that place and at that moment moved me to awe, to stillness; it moved me beyond words.

We watched the monkeys for a while longer, and I made several more attempts to capture what I could with my small camera-with-video, so I could share this wondrous sight back home.

Eventually we left the area and made our way back onto the open path. We were almost back to the water pumping station (low-tech and simple, the pump featured an open grate right there on the forest floor), when I felt a terrible, hot bite on my knee. I may have been moved beyond words a moment ago, but they came quickly in that moment: "OUCH! Something is biting my leg!!"

Josefu made a continuous motion with flat hands, the movement I was supposed to make but didn't understand fast enough, as I was focused on yanking up my pant leg.

The right move—just in case it happens to you—is to flat-cup your hands as though in upside-down prayer and, pointing them down to the ground, open them up then put them together again, clapping around the fabric of your clothes, while pulling the fabric away from your skin. Ideally, whatever is biting at you will be pulled away as well, for subsequent shaking to the ground.

I was instructed to remove my hiking boot. Josefu turned it upside down and out fell a red fire ant that had dropped into it from around my knee. They told me that these ants are much worse in the summer, and that they usually crawl up to the softest skin before they chomp down. I thought to myself, "thank goodness for chubby knees!"

For the rest of the trip, Honest would tease me, making pincer motions with his fingers, whenever we saw ants on the trail which, fortunately for me, was just a handful of times.

Inner Wisdom Lesson for me here: what a sublime example of how important it is to trust and listen to your intuition. When that sense-of-a-voice inside says, "Hey, maybe you shouldn't be standing here waiting for something to crawl up your pant leg." Well, maybe I should have honored my body's wisdom, taken heed and acted accordingly. Next time!

*   *   *

[From my notebook] *The drought here is severe. Elephants, zebras, wildebeests and other animals from nearby Kenya have crossed the border, searching for water. At night and early in the morning we heard neighboring farmers in the distance making noise—banging drums and shouting—to chase the elephants away from their farmed land, to save their hard-worked crops.*

There is a big contrast between small Chagga farms and these big farms. I passed pile after pile of nature's fertilizer on the Chagga lands; the big farms use pesticides and sprays. Simba Farm supplies lots of vegetables to the local market. They also supply beef and lamb. Here, you can buy a whole, live lamb for twenty dollars. You can buy a live chicken for four bucks. People pool their resources to buy a cow, and then, when enough families have contributed, the cow is slaughtered and the meat shared among them.

Next to the cattle stalls, I saw a tiny kitten that had stumbled out. It was far too young to be away from its mother, and the Massai who work with the cattle had given it milk in a plastic cap. I learned from Josefu that there were two puppies on the farm; one went into the woods with guests. Coincidentally (and completely unbeknownst to Josefu), the guests in this story were the four teachers I dined with at Mbahe Farm; they'd asked me to inquire about the farm's dogs, and now I understand why. The dog, in its curiosity, engaged the monkeys and then ran off, never to be seen again.

On our walk back to the farm Josefu and Honest taught me some Swahili:

Polé-Polé (pronounced po-lay po-lay), means "'slowly, slowly" and we would use this A LOT in the days ahead. *Asante sana* means "thank you," and its reply is *karibu sana*, "you're welcome." They taught me a variation on this: it is proper to say *shikamoo* when greeting an elder, to which the elder will respond, *marahaba*. I'm still not sure if these guys—both younger than me—were instructing me for when I'd meet my senior guide, Wilson, or if they wanted me to know how to respond if someone addressed me with *shikamoo*.

I learned the Swahili word for peacock: *Tausi (Ta-O-see)*, and this reminded me of the Sankofa Bird.

In April 2011, just before coming to Africa, I met Dr. Barbara Collins, at a lunchtime presentation, when she discussed her book, *It's your Turn: Find your Authentic Self and Go Fetch It.*

She asked the audience, "What would you be doing if you were not afraid?" I put down my utensils to grab a pen and make a note of that question.

Then she talked about the experience of looking back to her African roots in Ghana, her discovery of a symbol from the Akhan language of the Sankofa bird, and the philosophy it represents. The Sankofa bird is usually pictured looking backwards and the philosophy of it says: sometimes we need to look to the past in order to move forward. The Akan believe that the past illuminates the present and that the search for knowledge is a lifelong process.

(san = "to return") + (ko = "to go") + (fa = "to look, to seek and take")

"What would you be doing if you were not afraid?"

For me there were many answers to that question. At the time I scribbled it down, the answer was: to climb Mt. Kilimanjaro. To which I would add: If I were not afraid, I'd be brave enough to leave the country and all communication links, and the comforts of my home and my world, to traverse unknown-to-me East Africa. I would be courageous in the face of being away from home for a month while my mother was dying. I would let go and let be, let go of the need to be bossy, in control, and knowing all of the details. I would be able to let go of the need to be important in the process of her care and treatment. I would let myself off the hook of that story because I was the only one listening to it, and the others of my family didn't want to hear it.

What would I be doing if I were not afraid? Well, I'd let it be, as my Mom asked. I'd acknowledge, that even though I didn't know about every detail of her care, that it was okay, that she was happy with it most of the time, and that if she wasn't, her husband and other first daughter would take care of it. If I were not afraid, I would remove myself, literally, physically, from a very tense and incredibly sad time in our family, knowing that it was absolutely best for everyone that I make that move.

*   *   *

At Simba Farm, we had dinner at a big wooden table, on an open air porch. The table was prepared with a bounty of good food; served on charming, sturdy old china platters and in bowls that certainly would have stories to tell, if they could. Dinner was family-style and the foods were delicious. I wish I could remember now what we ate but I cannot. The feeling of the meal remains though; it felt like Thanksgiving as we passed heaping plates around the table. I do remember one item, the peas, and I remember commenting on how good they were. Our host agreed, and wondered aloud why the locals preferred hard peas instead of these soft but firm, fresh green peas. I ate them up.

The sun set and the evening came to an end. We all retired to our quarters and I seemed to be all alone in the big guest house. I walked out onto the front porch to marvel at the sky—the pink-hued remnants of the day left a blanket of stars in their wake. In a big, hardwood and mosquito-netted four-poster bed, I fell asleep to sounds of distant farmers banging drums and pans. I imagined their torches lit throughout the night as they worked furiously to ward off big, hungry elephants, and to protect the produce they had worked even harder to cultivate to feed their families.

DAY 4

Taking my final shower, before many days ahead where I wouldn't be able to, I was nonetheless wishing the water was warmer. We were at 5,800 feet of elevation after all, and the morning air was brisk. I dried off, brushed my teeth and combed out my hair, dressed, tied on my trusty hiking boots (so expertly broken in with extra help from the shoe store back home), and went out to look for my guides. We filled the water bottles, and Honest helped me fill and seal the CamelBak bladder[9], which I'd have a chance to use today.

My bags were packed for the trail. CamelBak, wet weather gear and a few essentials in the backpack, sleeping bag and bedroll, and most of my other items (efficiently compacted in big, zippered plastic bags, of course) were inside the body bag-sized duffel.

It was time to leave Simba Farm, travel to Londorossi Gate, and from there to Big Tree Camp. Our host had already begun his work for the day—days start early on such a big farm—so I wasn't able to extend my thanks for the hospitality. Nonetheless, I felt strong, prepared, and excited that day, thinking "Finally, today, we will begin to trek in earnest."

[From my SENE itinerary] *Londorossi Gate (6,890') to Big Tree Camp (8,700'), 3.8 miles. "After breakfast we drive to Londorossi Gate, where you will meet your other guides and mountain crew and enter the Kilimanjaro National Park. From the trailhead we walk for a few hours uphill through the thick and undisturbed montane forest to our camp for the night. Many beautiful flowers are seen en route and with luck we will observe*

---

[9] CamelBak is the brand. They invented a personal hydration system that combines a food-grade plastic balloon (the bladder), which fits into many backpacks. It's sized to hold up to 100 ounces of water, which the wearer can access through a tube that pops out in the front of the backpack. It is excellent for hands-free hydration.

Colobus monkeys and possibly signs of elephant. In the evening you may hear the unforgettable shrieking call of the tree hyrax."

As we made our way in the Land Rover, a baboon family crossed the red-dirt road, safely, in front of us. They moved quickly to the safety of the woods on the other side, but not before I had a chance to get a good look at the whole family. They peeked out from behind the brush as we drove by.

The sun was shining and the air was crisp and clear. We left the trees and soon were greeted by a big, blue sky dotted with puffy white clouds, and wide open fields. It looked and felt like a perfect weather day was ahead of us.

We met the team at the gate and checked in. I met Wilson, my other guide, and the whole crew. Honest and I signed in at the Ranger's desk. Everyone's bags were weighed to be sure the load was evenly distributed and that our porters weren't being asked to carry anything above the legal limit of 20 kilograms. My duffel—the one a porter will carry for me—squeaked in at just under the 20 kilogram limit (slightly more than 44 pounds) The backpack that I would be carrying, water-filled, weighed in at a measly 9.5 kilograms (just shy of 21 pounds).

I hopped into the Land Rover with Josefu and some of the team, while the rest piled into the second of our fully-loaded two-vehicle caravan. Higher and higher we climbed on dirt roads reminiscent of those around Mbahe Farm. It was a beautiful, sunny day and we saw groups of farmers and workers in fields along the way. The workers were using hand-held machetes to chop down the tall grasses alongside the road, making it wider in advance of the busy tourist season that would begin in earnest in just a few weeks. The felled grass served to fill in some of the pot holes, which, you might imagine, would cushion the passage, but it wasn't that soft. I grabbed on to the OJB—the "oh Jesus! bar"—to steady myself as we dipped into and out of some considerably deep divots.

Occasionally we stopped the cars so the drivers could make manual adjustments to the wheel hubs for what I'll call "superman" four-wheel drive, setting up the vehicle to get itself in-and-out of deep mud and potholes when necessary. It's that kind of road. Josefu said it was even more critical when the roads were wet. He also said that it wasn't uncommon for groups to walk up this 30-minute-by-car stretch of road, dry or wet. I've seen pictures of Land Rovers stuck in the mud on the road and (a) cannot imagine what it must be like to drive on this road during the rainy season, or to walk up it in rain and mud, and (b) think, how glad I am that we aren't walking up it today. If there is such a thing as guilty gratitude, then that's what I felt: ready to hike but grateful for the ride.

Eventually we came to a muddied-out stretch of road in deep woods, and Josefu declared that this was the end of the road for the Land Rovers. The trailhead was close, he told me, and so we could walk from here. I was surprised and sad when he said that he wouldn't be coming with us on the climb; someone had to drive the Land Rovers back, after all. So I gave him a hug, thanked him for keeping me safe, and strapped on my backpack. Eventually, everyone was out of the Land Rovers and making their way along the path. I waved goodbye to Josefu and then turned to follow the others.

The pack felt good on my back, my legs were happy to be moving on their own steam, and I settled in for what could be a long walk since I had no idea how many hours ahead camp would be. Finally we were beginning the trek in earnest—it was time for the climb to begin!

We were literally just a few hundred feet from where we'd left the Land Rovers when the men stopped. At the other side of a small clearing I could see the trailhead. They put down their bags and gear, and started to make lunch! I was ready to go but the food the chef and team had prepared was too good to resist so what's a girl to do but sit at the Kikoi[10]-covered table and say, "Asante sana."

Lunch was enough food for four people—sandwiches, fresh vegetables (carrots, cucumber, tomato), and tropical fruits (banana, mango, papaya). I chose to drink my bottled water instead of fruit juice. I ate what I wanted and could, and then asked Wilson if any of the men would help by eating the rest.

The team would pack up from lunch, Honest and Wilson informed me. Meanwhile, we three would pack up and hit the trail. I was beyond ready to go and did not want to appear impatient. I wanted to enjoy the day and go with the flow, but I was very happy that we were actually, surely, and most certainly heading out to walk on the trail now. I strapped on my backpack and crossed the clearing to the beginning of the trail.

The walk in and up was an easy one. Wilson was in the lead, then me, then Honest. The rest of the team packed up after lunch, and then trotted past us with their bulky loads, to set up camp ahead.

[From my notebook] *On the Hike—Day One—There's something to be said for this polé-polé leisurely approach to life and to trekking—I'm never winded and have a chance to see so much! Beautiful flowers, pink impatiens, purple thistle, green clover, deep blue-yellow-and-white pansies, vibrant red and yellow "elephant flowers." Today we saw small baboons cross the road as we left Simba farm, more Blue monkeys—closer this time—and Colobus monkeys (so beautiful!) on the trail, and a big glistening black bird that flashed red under its wings when it flew off. Stunning.*

There were plenty of people at Big Tree Camp when we arrived, including some children in a tent just next to mine. They were

---

[10] Kikoi is a plaid cotton cloth from Kenya, about three feet wide and five feet long, with fringed edges. I brought home several as gifts and kept one for our home. They're pretty, useful and I love plaid.

noisily enjoying their arrival, so I wandered over to a quieter part of the camp for some peace.

I found a small clearing almost completely surrounded by trees. It was obviously "camp" for other visitors who might arrive later, or on another day. The grass there was long and tamped down, making for a lush, cool and quiet space with a peek through the canopy of trees to the clouds in the sky. It was a late winter day in Africa and though the temperature wasn't what I'd call wintry (I was wearing just a long sleeve t-shirt and fleece vest), the light of the day certainly reflected what I experience in late fall-early winter at home.

It was just me and my thoughts in that peaceful place, at that quiet time. The quality of the light, the smell of woods and long grass, the color of the sky as I looked up through the ring of trees—it all reminded me of home. I felt a familiar heaviness in my heart, a reminder that it was still with me. I thought about Mom, Alan, Karen, and let the tears fall; I allowed myself to be with the feeling of homesickness and doubt, for just a couple of minutes. Then, I reminded myself to look immediately forward to what was sure to be a grand adventure.

Afternoon tea was served for me only, on a small folding table covered by a bright, cheery Kikoi. Although tea was solo, I had company for other meals. One of the guides joined me; they took turns sharing a meal with me so I didn't dine alone. One dined with me, the other with the men—for now anyway. When we got higher and it became colder, they'd let me eat in the mess tent, but I would still be served a separate meal and it would always be served first, which took some getting used to.

Though I'd hoped I could be "just one of the guys," I was beginning to understand the social and cultural dynamic between the men and me. Like it or not, in their minds, I was the client, and they were there to work for me. Wilson said, "Deb, it is my job to do all that I can to make sure you realize your dream of reaching the summit."

I was slow to realize and accept it, but eventually I came around to it. This was a professional climbing team, there to do their jobs and to do them well. Though I did come to accept it, I will admit that, it wasn't easy at all to simply allow myself to be taken care of.

*   *   *

Tea at Big Tree Camp

We were early to arrive at Big Tree Camp, so there was enough time for a walk after tea and before dinner. I followed Honest down a trail, and then we turned around and headed back up again. Along the way he taught me about some of the plants, flowers and birds of Kilimanjaro. Honest is well-studied and takes his profession seriously. As a senior guide he is well-versed in the flora and fauna of Kilimanjaro and the region, and he provided the Latin and scientific categorizations and histories of the living things we saw along the trail.

I hadn't consulted the book or my notes at this point, choosing instead to go with the flow and take it one day at a time, but I remembered reading something about unique animal sounds at Big Tree Camp, so I asked Honest about it. He told me that I'd hear barking dogs, or did he say laughing birds? I asked him to repeat it but I remained unclear at the time; I resolved that I would probably be able to tell which it was—dogs or birds— when and if I heard the sound.

[From my notebook] *We're at camp now, Big Tree Camp in the rain forest, and I'm feeling good. The sun is setting and it's chilly, but dinner will be served soon—another feast of corn and sweet potato soup, peanut chicken stew, brown rice, green beans and mushrooms, finished with fruit salad. They even found tree tomatoes for me! That and passion fruit at lunch with meat and cheese, loads of organic veggies and fruits, bread, avocado. Life is good. And very delicious.*

There was a fancy, typed menu on night number one in camp, which was a considerate touch. After that, Wilson and Honest would tell me what we were having, translating from the chef's Swahili. All the men on the team spoke Swahili. Only my guides, Wilson and Honest, spoke English.

Despite a physical day, sleep was slow to come, mostly thanks to the dancing flashlights and giggles of the kids next door. Though their enjoyment was delightful, I was craving space to be alone with my thoughts and enjoy the sounds of this incredible place undisturbed.

The next day, I asked my guides to build our camp as far away from others as they could, whenever it was possible, just for some peace and quiet. From that day onward, my sleeping and latrine tents were together, apart from the men and away from others in camp. That is, when there were others in camp.

DAY 5

Early the next morning I heard it. Disorienting at first, but because of what I'd read I wasn't surprised to hear inhuman sounds very early in the morning at Big Tree Camp. I could not imagine, for the life of me, how dogs could make such sounds, over such distance, as though they were in the trees. The low throaty sound was unique. I'd not heard anything else like it, and the acoustics in that camp were amazing!

When I was a small girl, we had big stereo speakers in the family room, and a turntable. I loved to listen to Dad's records, dance and sing into a make-believe microphone. I was Donna Summer. I was both Simon & Garfunkel. I loved the acoustics in the song *Baby Driver* from the *Bridge Over Troubled Water* album (Simon & Garfunkel), especially the part with the sound of a revved-up race car engine, that moved from one speaker to the next. When I closed my eyes, it was as though the car drove right past me. THAT is how these barking dogs/laughing birds sounded—as though they were in one ear and then the next. Forget surround sound . . . this was old fashioned hi-fi stereo, with the volume turned up.

How big a bird would this have to be to generate such a powerful call? I tried to find an Internet recording but could not; if you want to know what the morning sounds like at Big Tree Camp on Mt. Kilimanjaro, you'll just have to go there.

Even after I read the passage in Stedman's book again and knew what it was, I remained stupefied by those big sounds. They were not barking dogs or laughing birds after all—the actual name was lost in translation yesterday, or, more accurately, lost by my inaccurate hearing.

The tree hyrax is a small, furry, round, rodent-looking herbivore the size of a large guinea pig, about 20 inches long and weighing three to five pounds. It's a distant relative of the elephant, if you can believe it, (I can't), and no, I still can't figure out how I heard barking dog or laughing bird from tree hyrax either.

I never saw them, only heard them; they were loud and clear. One will answer the call of another as families reassemble after going out to eat at night. Hyrax calls combine different sounds: they are a raucous nocturnal shriek that starts as a squeak, then rises to a squeal and finally to a scream, as they ascend and descend in the trees. Their acoustics were fascinating and multi-directional, as though they were in the tree just next to the tent, then farther away, and then quickly back again.

The unforgettable shrieking call of the tree hyrax is unlike anything I've ever heard, and I didn't hear it again on any other night, not even on the way out.

*   *   *

[From my SENE itinerary] *Big Tree Camp (8,700') to Shira 1 Camp (11,420'), 4.7 miles. "Today we reach the west side of the Shira Plateau in a hiking time of 6 hours. Taking our time walking through the forest allows us to observe its animal and bird life. The day's hike takes us from the montane forest, through a transition zone, and into the heath zone, where old lava flows are visible. Your guides will point out unique environmental differences that characterize each zone. After a picnic lunch we reach the edge of the Plateau and eventually our camp that offers a dramatic view of Kilimanjaro and its permanent glaciers."*

It was a glorious walk and the pictures are proof that, by some miracle, my hair still looked good—even though I didn't think so at the time. We were rising above the rain forest at an easy pace and the vista was broadening; we looked down into wide

A good hair day

gulleys of trees and tropical plants.

On this day, I had some important lessons in patience, which started when those little energy ball kids zoomed past us on the trail. Being the mature adult that I am, I wanted to move faster too, but Wilson maintained the leisurely, polé-polé pace in front, blocking my way.

Poor Wilson, I'm sure this happens to him all the time: I was almost breathing on his backpack in my desire to move faster, but when we got to camp, he explained his strategy: travel at too fast a pace and you'll flame out (my words). He said, "Trust me, because I've seen it so many times. Those kids will be tired, feel sick and start whining in a day." We didn't see them again after Shira I Camp, so I don't know what happened, but I do know that I trusted the wisdom and experience of my guide.

The polé-polé pace was a lesson. On one hand, it was nice. Sometimes. I enjoyed having the time to look around and to have the luxury to notice what was all around me. I enjoyed it a lot in reality, because it was refreshingly different for me, the one who is used to watching her feet and moving quickly. But other times that polé-polé pace was a challenge. It isn't easy to go slowly when you're used to moving at a different, faster pace. When I hike with my family, we move quickly. The boys (Alan included) have always been able to run circles around me; they all move at a much more rapid pace than I do, and I've always felt like the big slow-poke in comparison.

In ten years as a family with a preference for mountain hiking vacations (the boys have been skiing since they were two years old and love the mountains all year round), we've been to the western U.S. (Idaho, Colorado) and western Canada (Banff to Jasper), the Matterhorn in Zermatt, the Dolomites in Italy, Norway, New Zealand, and the Appalachian Trail in Maine, Vermont and Pennsylvania.

I've always felt the need to prove to them that I can keep up. Over Christmas 2010, we were together in Patagonia. We had beyond-perfect weather and enjoyed stunningly beautiful hikes. It was on one of these hikes that, after ten years of marriage and lots of hiking vacations together, Alan declared "Hey, you're really a hiker."

I shared this story—that I've always worked hard to keep up with Alan, Chip and Mike—with our friend, Al Chaby, who responded, "Deb, you're not easy to keep up with." I'd never thought of it that way.

[From my notebook] *We left the rain forest and saw a few more Colobus monkeys on our way. A Blue monkey kept me company, as though on lookout, while I found a private spot behind some trees to pee. We headed to moorland, to Shira plateau, where we were rewarded with the first glimpse of Kili, only partially obscured by clouds. By the time I settled in at camp, she was completely cloud-covered and the clouds rolled in just above us.*

Coming in to camp this afternoon I was greeted by the whole porter crew who sang and danced and clapped and welcomed me to the base of the mountain. Man o man do these porters work hard. My pack is 9.5 kilograms loaded with H_2O—they carry 20 kilograms each. They pass us on the trail and we step aside to let them go by with their wide, heavy loads. Honest clasps his hands and looks down as they go by, as if to bless their safe passage.

Along this part of the trail I noticed a dusty cluster of sticks and stones, and remembered a saying from childhood, "Sticks and stones may break my bones, but names will never hurt me." I was moved to capture it on film. It looked like the dusty old bones of an animal feast.

Arriving at Shira 1—here is where my second and last pen ran out of ink (I lost the first one somehow somewhere). I am now writing with a pen I borrowed from Wilson.

Today I saw the peak for the first time. Climbing uphill through terrain that was changing from forest to moorland, I could see clearly all the way across the Shira plateau (looks like a wide valley) to the peak of Mt. Kilimanjaro. I had to pause for a minute, slow the walking and let out a few tears as emotion took over. I cannot believe that I am actually here and I feel incredibly humbled by the majesty of what appears before me.

Remember that quote, "What lies before us and behind us are nothing compared to what lies within us?" Well, today, I am reminded of that quote. I feel connected to this place and about to begin a wonder-full[11] relationship with this mountain; I feel like it is she who has allowed me to be here.

That quote, from Ralph Waldo Emerson, is another that accompanied me on this journey, because it's one of my favorites. I have it framed in my office at home, on a card I received from my step-mother Norma. It serves as a reminder to me in difficult times.

Shira I Camp was crowded, or rather it appeared more so because we were out of the wooded area and the terrain was much more exposed. Also, three trails—Shira, Lemosho and Machame, and the people trekking on them—meet there, then diverge again. We'll be breaking away from the "crowds" soon.

Meanwhile, the camp was active and there was plenty to watch. We saw the little kids, who were much quieter. I watched their parents doing yoga, tree pose. A group of young trekkers was playing Frisbee. There was good, fun energy around us in camp, which I enjoyed. I also enjoyed, thanks to my trusty porter team,

---

[11] Intentional spelling. I was full of wonder at what I saw there, and this sense of being full of wonder was, indeed, a companion each day.

the privacy offered by the placement of our tents, which were on the edge of camp.

Low-hanging clouds converged on camp in the late afternoon and without the sun it quickly became cold and damp. But they rolled out again later at night and I know this because I got up in the wee hours of the morning to go to the bathroom (with chattering teeth) and to stare at the sky.

DAY 6

A lot of people believe there are special places on the planet, "energetic hot spots," where a swirling funnel of subtle energy comes from within the earth up to the surface, and it's palpable to people within its range.

Native Americans gave spiritual significance to these energetic hot spots where they found them, and several were identified in Sedona, Arizona, for example. It was in Sedona where I learned about this natural phenomenon known as a *vortex*.

Travelling with girlfriends, we endeavored to find at least one of the seven vortexes of Sedona, and to see what all the fuss was about. We made our way to one spot that was supposed to be a vortex but didn't feel anything. It was anti-climactic. Could it be a bunch of hooey?

On the way out of the park we stopped in a Frank Lloyd Wright building, the Church in the Rock. It was sunny and beautiful outside, and in contrast, cool, quiet and still inside. Walking down the aisle toward the altar I was suddenly, briefly, overwhelmed with emotion. It happened in a particular spot, about three-quarters of the way down the aisle from the doorway, a brief sensation like walking through a short space of cool on a hot day. And I had that same feeling—a sweep of emotions briefly and all at once—on the way back toward the door, at that same spot.

It was only later that I learned the Church in the Rock is considered by some to be the eighth vortex in Sedona.

When I woke up the next day in Shira 1 Camp, it was a glorious morning. I sat at the table while Honest checked my vital signs[12] and, breathing normally for an accurate reading, I closed my eyes to enjoy feeling the warmth of the sun on my face.

---

12 Blood oxygen level, pulse and breaths per minute were measured twice daily.

All of a sudden that vortex feeling hit me: I was overwhelmed by gratitude, by the grace and beauty of this place, so thankful that I was there, sensing that the mountain was granting me permission to come here, to be here, for healing, for my soul. It felt like a big hug, as if she patted me gently on the back saying softly, "You come here, child. Everything is going to be fine." Big tears came freely, rolling down my cheeks, slowly, and I let them. Honest must be familiar with clients who have emotional moments because he gracefully left me alone with mine.

It was as though she was speaking to me in her own language and mine. *Karibou* is Swahili for "she welcomes you."

I know it sounds dramatic, but it's what I felt and it was overwhelming. I am emotionally moved still when retelling this part of the story because it comes from deep within my heart, from the place where I hold the memory of the mountain; remembering the emotions of it are so very much a part of my experience, and they are with me forever.

I believe that Mt. Kilimanjaro is a vortex.

*   *   *

[From SENE Itinerary] *Shira 1 Camp (11,420') to Shira 2 Camp (12,750'), 5.3 miles. "Today is an easy paced acclimatization day of 4 to 5 hours hiking. Camp is set higher on the Shira Plateau with more expansive views of Kilimanjaro. There is a conditioning hike in the afternoon where you can examine the clusters of giant lobelias and senecios that grow at this elevation."*

I packed up the contents of my tent, rolled the sleeping bag and pad, stuffed every squashable thing into a giant ziplock, and then lay across it to expel the air. So efficient! I was always so proud of myself when my bag was packed up and ready for the porter team. I left the giant duffel in the tent for the porter team to collect later and went outside, with my backpack and water bottles, for filling.

At the end of the day's hike, Wilson let me walk fast across the Shira plain, just as we were approaching Shira 2. I *really* had to go to the bathroom and we were *so* close, so I pleaded my case. It was a straight shot, he could see me the entire way, and to my relief he gave me the go ahead. I know, I know that I'm supposed to be going slowly, slowly, but it sure did feel good to move it, move it!

I decided at this point to just give up on the pens that I kept losing, and on writing notes. I turned instead to my trusty mini-recorder for the rest of the trek, except for writing post cards at Lava Tower Camp (with a reclaimed pen).

My recordings, like the transcriptions from my notes, are typed and *shown in italics*. Let me apologize to you now: the dates may be out of sync and I beg your indulgence as I sometimes repeat myself along the way. Let's chalk it up to altitude, okay?

[From my recording] *Phase 3, Day 3 with a new pen. I began this trip with two pens, a primary and a backup. I lost them both. Then, I borrowed one from Wilson. At this point I have lost the one I borrowed but found one of my originals. Perhaps I am not supposed to be writing? So I will record.*

Sitting at Shira 2 after a morning walk in to camp. Lunch was grilled cheese, tomato and onion sandwiches, pumpkin soup with lots of cut veggies, fruits and hot tea. Always good. Last night's dinner was enjoyed in the mess tent with chef Katunzi, sous chef China, waiter Robby.

Right now I'm sitting on a rock with a white collared raven for company and an outstanding view of the mountain. The team welcomed me to camp with song today, telling me in Swahili that I am fit and strong and doing an outstanding job, which makes me smile. I think I have Watu Azuri—the best team.

I had a mild headache yesterday at 8,000 feet, and my hands were tingly after washing them in hot water. Today my feet were tingly too, the left more than the right. Wilson told me this was a side effect to expect with Diamox, the most tried and tested drug for altitude sickness prevention and treatment, which I am now taking twice a day. Since it's a known diuretic, Wilson suggested I take it in the morning with breakfast—I can make a pit-stop on the trail if I need to—and at lunch time. Taking it before dinner is not advisable, he says, because this increases the likelihood of needing to get up for the latrine throughout the night. I read about this. It was the experience of many others who've gone before me; they've written about the annoying side effect of constantly having to get up in the night and use the bathroom. No one wrote about the wisdom of taking the drug during the day only . . . thanks, Wilson, because this was propitious advice! I have to remember to tell Susan at Penn Travel Medicine so she can tell other Kili climbers.

Forgot to say that despite a couple of days of walking, my calves and joints feel surprisingly good . . . there is, admittedly and without doubt, something to this polé-polé. It works. Plus, I'm drinking a ton of water.

I have been moved to tears several times today—experiencing the sunset, the mountain, Wilson saying grace at lunch, thinking of Mom along the way. It's hard to believe I'm actually here. I'll be in the moment, then bam it hits me: Remember? You're in Africa!

The hikes on this day were rewarding, both the walk in and the afternoon acclimatization hike. In fact, the sun accompanied us for most of the day as we wandered past diverse local residents. Residents like the Giant Lobelias, which I saw in several stages of their development—from the uniformly unfolding low-to-the-ground green rosettes that spanned 12 inches or more, to the three-to-four foot-tall cones with weepy, triangular green leaves, inside of which I found perfect, tiny, white flowers.

We passed glorious Senecios that reminded me of Joshua Trees: 8 feet tall with dry, brown cactus-shaped bodies, elbowed arms reaching to the sky, and each holding a tuft of leafy green pom-pom on top.

I was repeatedly distracted by the shiny-flecked rocks glinting in the sun; they seemed to wink as I walked near, "Look at me! Look at me!" I was enthralled by the expansive cauliflower-looking clusters of white Helichrysum with golden centers—the dried-flower version of daisies.

[From my recording] *The flowers are like smiles. All the way, from the rain forest to the moorland, captivating plant life abounds. According to Honest, who has studied all of the flora and fauna of the mountain and surrounding area, there are actually just a few different species of plant, but there are many varieties of each.*

LOCAL RESIDENTS

Giant Lobelia

Senecios

Helichrysium

There were clouds above and below. It was incredibly windy and that, combined with our altitude, made the clouds look like they were moving fast. Big, fluffy white clouds sailed at a brisk pace across a bright blue sky. I was wearing the right gear to block the wind and being comfortable always helped to make it a splendid day on Mt. Kilimanjaro.

On the afternoon hike we looked back to the right, down and out across the plateau, where Honest pointed out clouds of dust rising from the long, seemingly empty road below. From our vantage point it looked small, like a dirt trail. But earlier we'd taken a break next to it, so I knew it was a dirt road, and almost two lanes wide as a matter of fact. It's a rescue road and unfortunately, someone was on it.

We continued forward on our acclimatization hike, travelling up the trail to a point where we were able to get a first glimpse of the wall around the crater and more specifically, the break in it known as the western breach. We were so far away from it that I couldn't get an exact reading on the trail, on how, precisely, we would be making it up that steep angle and across that entire loose-looking patch of mountain slide.

I believe growth happens when we're on the edge of our comfort zones. One thing I tell my clients, in the contract we both sign up front, is this: "Remember: when it feels like you want to throw in the towel, the real work is beginning. Make the commitment to yourself to stick with it. Your coach will encourage you; you can count on it." I didn't fully realize at the time that I was looking right at the edge of my comfort zone.

The sun was setting and the shadows were getting longer as we made our way back to camp. Walking in this direction provided an incredible look over an edge to the left, and a stunning view of the clouds far below. On a typical mountain hike I'd think we were above the clouds, but there was another layer of fluffy whites sailing overhead.

Honest explained the lower cloud ceiling was generated by the rainforest giving up its moisture. Very cool and something I'd never seen before. We made our way back down to camp where I had some time to record a few notes before dinner.

[From my recording] *Right now I'm in my tent and I'd like to record some tips.*

Tip #1: Bring a nail brush, that's what I would say, bring a nail brush! Bring something to clean your fingernails because you can't imagine how much dirt you get under them.

Tip #2: Wear your gaiters[13] to help with dust. I've always thought of them as something I'd use to keep snow out of my boots, and to keep my lower pant legs dry, but, to my surprise, they are definitely good for dust, so I will be putting them on tomorrow.

So, what else? Take as many days as you can. I'm on the nine day route and it most definitely does make quite a difference. And go slowly, slowly—polé-polé is what they say—because what a HUGE difference this makes. And drink plenty of water—this is what has made the journey so much more successful for me compared to past hikes I've taken.

Walking slowly and drinking a lot of water, I have no body aches and no cramping, no tight muscles, even at this elevation—we're just above 11K feet. It's been three days of hiking and I have to say I'm impressed with this whole approach.

Okay, 7:30 at night now, just had another delicious dinner and watched a peaceful, beautiful sunset. It's June 15th, 2011 so there is a full moon tonight and it's gorgeous! And the stars are out, but you know what? It is so damn cold that I can't stay outside so I'm in my tent, I'm putting on my super-thick wool socks and my feet are still cold and so are my hands and I still have my jacket on. But it's time to get ready for bed, to tuck into my sleeping bag, get toasty warm and do some reading.

---

[13] Gaiters are good for keeping legs and feet relatively clean and dry on the trail. They wrap around the leg from beneath the knee down and over the laces of the boot.

The higher we got on this trek, the colder it was at night. I brought Alan's sleeping bag, sized for a tall, thin man. It was warm but . . . as someone who likes to sleep sideways and curl up one leg or two, I was challenged by the narrow triangular-cocoon shape. Unzipping the bag aided mobility, but wasn't a good solution for keeping warm.

I added this to the list of things to do differently next time: bring a spacious, rectangular-shaped sleeping bag. Or two sleeping bags that can be zipped together. Or two sleeping bags plus one Alan. The down jacket served as an extra 'blanket' and I used my soft polyfill jacket as a pillow. For this trip it would have to do.

DAY 7

[From SENE Itinerary] *Shira 2 Camp (12,750') to Lava Tower Camp (15,230'), 4.3 miles. "Today is another important day for acclimatization as we hike for 5 hours to an elevation above 15,000 feet. We will pass through the alpine moorland zone where plants are extremely hardy and consist of lichens, grasses, and heather, to reach Kilimanjaro's alpine desert zone. After an early afternoon rest we have a special 2 hour SENE adventure climb up the Lava Tower. This rock scramble will prepare you for the climbs ahead."*

[From my recording] *So we arrived today at Lava Tower Camp which, according to Henry Stedman, is at 15,180 feet. We've gone up and down, had a nice dusty walk of about 4 ½ hours to get here and it's beautiful. We are the only people camping out. It's a favorite place for lunch for many folks but they've all gone on to other routes, and we are the only people camping here tonight.*

We're going to take a rest afternoon, which is welcomed. Although I have to say again that I feel remarkably well and I think it's got to be due to taking it slowly, polé-polé, and drinking a lot of water: There's no tightness in the calves, my hips feel good. I mean, the parts of my body that usually hurt actually are not a problem.

We're at the base of the western breach, which is the route that we'll be taking to the top, and tomorrow we'll be exploring this particular area. We're going to stay here for another day and night. From here I can see the path that we're going to take to get to the base of the western breach. We start climbing straight up from there. It's been a good day and I look forward to recording more.

*   *   *

Our camp was away from the craziness of the lunching crowds that had been directly beneath Lava Tower. My guides told me that Lava Tower is deteriorating, that it's not a safe scramble, yet the rowdy American-sounding English-speaking students were all over it, shouting at and to each other from its top. This was okay by me; I was happy to relax in camp.

The trails were dry and dusty and after coughing up trail dust for a day or so, I'd figured out that I needed to use a scarf or my lovely pink thin wool neck tube to filter the air I was breathing. I think I looked like a bank robber, but if it worked then at least I could breathe without coughing on the afternoon excursion. For those planning to walk these dusty trails, be prepared.

Before leaving home, I purchased lovely green-and-pink patterned quilt squares (chakra colors of the heart, plus they matched my jacket and backpack) at the local fabric store. I sewed rolled seams around two of them during the long airplane ride over so that I could use them as handkerchiefs. I looped one, sometimes two, in front of me through elastic bands at the top of the backpack straps for easy access. I thought they'd be useful as across-the-mouth wraps, if needed, to combat dust but that plan didn't work—they were too loose to be effective. So, bring your hankies and bring a neck tube too.

Something else I found helpful to carry with me on the trail: tissues and a ziplock baggie for pit stops. I read about and purchased the little plastic funnels that allow a woman to pee standing up. In my personal experience, they weren't ideal. This might have something to do with the fact that I tried to use mine while kneeling in my little tent in the middle of the night because it was so darned cold that I didn't want to go outside, but in the end, the "Shewee[14]" lost and the loo won.

When you're on the trail, the guides know where to direct you for privacy. You'll notice in many spots that others have been there

---

[14] One of several brands of these plastic funnels.

before you. Personally, I believe that what you pack in on a hike you must pack out. No exceptions. Wilson and I debated this point. He believes the tissue breaks down easily enough and can be left behind, but it hurts my heart to see it.

I used small zip jewelry bags, two inches by three inches, to store my daily vitamins and other pills (Diamox, anti-malarial), and then I recycled these little baggies for TP on the trail. I put the tissue into the ziplock baggie and then the whole thing went into the community trash bag.

*   *   *

At Lava Tower Camp, I found lava rocks all around. They look like ordinary gray rocks on the outside but inside, thanks to others who'd been at the campsite before me, and who had broken a few of the rocks into pieces, I could see that inside they are opaque, black, glassy obsidian.

I'd done some research into the healing properties of stones and crystals shortly after Mom was diagnosed and then went crazy buying beads from around the world. I took a few beading classes and bought the materials to make healing necklaces for my mom, my sisters and some girlfriends. In the face of what felt like an utterly hopeless situation, making "healing necklaces" was a way of coping, of doing something—anything.

Judy Hall's, *The Encyclopedia of Crystals*, was a go-to reference for me. It's where I found out about the healing properties of natural Obsidian, which I thought were fascinating. Black obsidian doesn't have a crystalline structure; therefore, it has no boundaries or limitations. It can help a person assimilate things that are hard to accept; it supports emotional clarity by helping to see beyond one's self-limiting beliefs. She describes black obsidian as a stone that "forces facing up to one's true Self, taking you deep into the subconscious mind, magnifying negative energies so that they can be fully experienced and released."

According to her, black obsidian's effect on one's perception of power serves to redefine it, reaching back through ancestral ties and family lines with a healing effect

Now this is my kind of rock, because power issues are another one of my special gifts. I've received a lot of feedback about having a powerful presence with the potential to overwhelm. I and others in my world could only benefit from my being better at managing that, so whether or not you believe in the power of crystals, I had to try it. You never know.

I was entranced by the rocks I found at Lava Tower Camp. Formed from molten lava over 360,000 years ago, they were bewitching.

I learned from Honest that the summit is getting shorter, closer to sea level. He thinks it's because so many people take rocks from the summit. So I decided that this team should do its part to rebuild the mountain and selected a few stones to bring to the top. One for Honest and one for me, I was determined to symbolically contribute to the rebuilding of the summit. I tucked one extra piece into my bag to take home and though I could not in the moment decide which of the three pieces it would be, I didn't have to just yet, and tucked them all into my backpack.

One piece now sits with me on my desk at home and, since obsidian is a powerful stone, I hold it when I feel the need for clarity.

*   *   *

I should mention that our weather continued to be truly delightful. No rain and the days were bright and sunny. It was so nice, that I thought I might be able to get some wash done.

When we arrived into camp, I asked about washing some key items of clothing. I'd seen the men lay their clothes on the sun-warmed rocks for airing out and fast drying. Honest offered that the men would be happy to wash my clothing for me, but I respectfully declined—I'd read in Stedman's guidebook that it's impolite to ask another person to wash your undergarments and I didn't want to be rude.

They gave me a small washtub along with a huge bucket of warm water—water that had to be carried up from the stream and then heated on our small stove in batches—and a square of industrial soap for clothes washing.

I had only a few pair of Smartwool underwear and some socks that I was willing to risk getting wet. I decided that the rest, shirts and non-wool socks/undies, could wait.

Smartwool is a highly recommended purchase—it wicks and breathes, plus washes and dries out in a flash. I discovered the Ice Breaker line of it in New Zealand and will never go back to polypropelene or other unnatural fiber athletic clothing again. Famed for its 'no stink' qualities, it airs out quickly and helps to regulate body temperature as only wool can, in my experience. To me, it's like cashmere in that regard, but a lot sturdier.

It may be irresponsible to tell you this part, but I'm going to anyway. Thanks to the polé-polé pace (and maybe to my smart Smartwool wardrobe?), I didn't break a sweat on this climb. Seriously.

I stocked up on several layers of Ice Breaker and Smartwool for this trip: two lightweight shirts, one short-sleeved and one long-sleeved, a heavier weight shirt with thumb loops, which are ideal for hiking since they help protect your hands from sunburn (didn't save my thumbs, but more on that later).

I also splurged on a better-fitting pair of long underwear, a pair of heavier-weight pants (that I have worn so much I bought another pair as soon as I got back to the U.S.) and three pair of underwear (I would have had more, one for each day, but they were expensive).

Thick wool hiking socks are a must, but most hikers already know this part. I wore two pair each day, taking them off in the afternoons when I got to camp, and beating them on a rock to get the dust out. I rotated them once each and wore them to bed at night before they were retired from the rotation. The opportunity to wash a couple pair was a luxury.

On our way in to camp today, I met some interesting people as we kept exchanging lead on the path. I would stop for a break, they would pass, they would stop for a break, and I would pass. To one of the women I had to say, "Your hair looks so clean! You must have cheated." She assured me that she, like me, had not showered or washed her hair for a few days now.

I was stupefied by the outsized cameras two of the men were carrying—seemed to me to be a lot of weight. One in the group took my photo and later, when it was my turn to pass them on the trail, he gave me his business card.

Karsten Delap is a professional mountain guide and photographer, which explained the camera. I have one of his photos as my laptop screen saver and appreciate the perspective it provides of me and my guides on the dusty trail approaching sub-alpine terrain, well above the rainforest clouds.

When we arrived at camp, I was thinking not only about washing my clothes but also of washing my hair. It was another beautiful, sunny day after all, with a breeze that, though on the cool side, would make for quick-drying hair in the sun.

I mentioned this to Honest, adding that I didn't plan to be able to wash my hair on the trail and so didn't bring shampoo with me. "Oh, you need shampoo?" he said, "Sure, I have some shampoo!" I thought this was serendipitous—I was indeed going to get to wash my hair—what a break. Seeing my expression, Honest started to chuckle and passed his hand over his head. Honest has a very, very short haircut and doesn't need shampoo at all.

Undeterred, I decided to use the block of industrial-strength clothes soap and prayed that my hair wouldn't fall out as a result. Note to self for next time: pack a small single-use sample of shampoo. Of course, if you pack it in, you may not have a sunny day on which to use it, but you never know what Mother Nature will deliver and it's best to be prepared.

I was incredibly mindful of the work it took to carry water up from the stream below and to warm it on the tiny gas stove, so I used it sparingly, rinsing my hair with the smallest of cupfuls. I carefully allowed the runoff water to fall back into the dirty water bin that I would then be able to use for my feet after.

My hair dried in the wind and it was a refreshing feeling to have clean-again hair. At first. By evening however, I realized that I hadn't washed all of the industrial soap out, so my hair was weighted down and greasy looking.

*   *   *

Later in the afternoon I walked across the area from our camp, on one side, to the base of Lava Tower on the other. There I found a nice wall of rocks that formed a high ledge, with a big, 30 foot drop off on the side that looked back over the trail we'd come in on.

The sun was setting, the shadows were long and it was quiet since the lunch crowds had broken down and moved on along their routes to the North. They would most likely be sleeping in huts tonight, according to the direction I believed their trail to be heading in. It would not be our direction; we were heading to the West, through the breach.

Sitting there on the wall, I watched the white-necked ravens rise and swoop, on patrol for their evening meal.

I brought to this spot several post cards and stamps, which I'd previously purchased in Arusha with the help of Josefu, when we'd stopped there before heading to Simba Farm. I wrote each one out and addressed them to my nephews and to Mom in

Pennsylvania, to my sister in Florida, to Dad and Judy and to Norma and Joe in New York, and to Uncle Don and Kit in California. I selected one with a lioness on a rock and addressed it for home:

> *Dear Athena (my dog) & everyone else, Today we arrived at Lava Tower 12,180' and I feel remarkably well. Drinking 2.5-3 litres of water each day and walking polé-polé (slowly slowly) is the trick. When I say slowly you can't imagine; I haven't broken a sweat since we left the rain forest on days 1-2. And they keep making me eat! Soup, fruit, veggies—organic and all good. With love, Deb*

I missed my family. Sitting alone on that perch, I missed home. Feeling the loss of the energy from the lunch crowd, my mood was melancholy. I was homesick, feeling lonely, and so I went back to camp and tried again to call home.

Attempts to reach the States by phone were comical. Despite taking care to protect the charge in the batteries, to have extra batteries, to keep them warm and dry and the extra effort to obtain a SIM card in Kenya that was "guaranteed to work in Tanzania" (what was I thinking?!), the calls just would not go through.

One of the first activities the men did upon arriving at any camp was to walk around to the highest places to try to get a signal. Honest was able to connect with the office just about each day and the men with their families. But not me.

We kept trying to call each afternoon; Wilson even let me try his phone, but the results were the same, no connection. Despite the constant companionship of my guides during the days, and eating in a tent with the team of ten in the evenings, I felt alone. I wanted to hug my dog, to share some of this experience with the people I cared about the most. I missed my family. I missed home.

DAY 8

[From SENE itinerary] *Lava Tower Camp (15,230'). "We spend a second night at Lava Tower to adjust to the high desert environment, taking day hikes to higher elevations and marveling at the stark yet magnificent vistas up and down the massif. As with every day on the mountain, the guides twice daily measure your vital signs, including oxygen saturation, to assess your acclimatization to the extreme altitude."*

Honest would get my vitals before dinner in the evenings and over breakfast each morning, until it got very cold, and then he'd "knock" on my tent in the mornings to get my vital signs.

You can see from the chart that I was doing well so far. I was extremely pleased with my oxygen (O_2) levels because it was (and still is) my belief that high O_2 numbers mean no AMS. I attributed the "good scores" to the Diamox and the Chlorophyll, both of which I took religiously, twice a day.

My vital statistics up to this point are on the next page.

You can see the complete version of "My Kilimanjaro Report Card," from beginning to end, at the end of this story.

Client Vitals Sheet for Deb Denis, Female, Age 46, Height: 5', 6"
Weight (*you didn't think I'd put THAT in here, did you?*)

		Elevation (Feet)	O2 Saturation (%)	Heart Rate (BPM)	Respiration breath/min	Water Intake (litres)	Diamox 250mgx2	Location	Other
11-Jun-11	AM	6000	95	70	9			Mbahe Farm	
11-Jun-11	PM	6000	96	73	8			Mbahe Farm	
12-Jun-11	AM	6000	96	84	9		x	Mbahe Farm	
12-Jun-11	PM	5800	97	76	8	2	x	Simba Farm	
13-Jun-11	AM	5800	95	70	7.5		x	Simba Farm	
13-Jun-11	PM	8700	92	79	8	2.5	x	Big Tree Camp	
14-Jun-11	AM	8700	93	78	8		x	Big Tree Camp	
14-Jun-11	PM	11420	89	74	7	3	x	Shira 1	light headache; naproxen x2
15-Jun-11	AM	11420	87	72	8		x	Shira 1	
15-Jun-11	PM	12750	88	72	7	3	x	Shira 2	
16-Jun-11	AM	12750	90	77	8.5		x	Shira 2	
16-Jun-11	PM	15230	85	81	9	3.5	x	Lava Tower	light headache; naproxen x2
17-Jun-11	AM	15230	85	74	8		x	Lava Tower	

[From my recording] *It's the morning of day 5 and it is damn cold. My hands are freezing and I just can't get them warm enough; I think I've made a critical error in not bringing warm enough gloves even though I have two pair. My feet are extremely cold too.*

But it's beautiful here and in the middle of the night, at around 2 a.m. when the winds die down and I get up to use the bathroom, the skies are clear and it's JUST gorgeous. The moon is full and so the stars don't show themselves against the full moon; you have to catch them before the moon comes up over the mountain, which we were able to do last night. And then of course the sky is dense with them, but it's too cold to stay outside long enough to look at them for very long.

I wanted to make some notes on the team, what I've come to know about them over the past few days on the trail and at camp.

Each day there are philosophical debates along the way between Wilson and my chief/head guide Honest Matto. Honest is a devout Christian, 35 years old, a very gentle man who at one time gave serious consideration to entering the priesthood. I learned yesterday that his wife's name is Beatrice and that they have two little girls, Jacqueline, who is 5, and Diana, who is 3.

Wilson Moshe is the assistant guide and he has over a thousand summits. He is 66 years old and very knowledgeable. The men have a lot of respect for him and he's very well known to others we pass on the trail. He is quite a philosopher and all topics are rooted in the Bible, as he's Christian, and very religious. He said to me on day 2, "You know, basically, this is where I come from, this is where my conversation will come from, and I hope that it won't bother you. Let me have my faith and I won't try to change yours." So that was how he started it off; my guess is that he's had conversations with other clients about that in the past.

I told Wilson that I consider myself to be a deeply spiritual person. I'd been exposed to many belief systems, though mostly

Judeo-Christian, through my own life's experiences—Protestant, Catholic, Methodist, Southern Baptist, Armenian and Greek Orthodox, and several levels of Judaism; I'd heard the call to prayer in many cities I'd travelled in. All that said, I'm not a follower of any particular organized religion. I know that a person's religion can be very much a part of how they define themselves, as in Wilson's case; his faith is strong and forms an important foundation for him, which is where conversation stems from. I told Wilson that as long as it wasn't proselytizing I didn't mind it at all.

So, one of the reasons I picked up the tape recorder was to record some notes from last night's conversation. All conversations with Wilson are philosophical; he challenges the men to think. There is good debate around the topics and I wonder if that's part of the trekking team culture—I like it. It's a way to discover different perspectives and learn to respect other opinions.

Last night's discussion over dinner was about faith. Honest posed a question: do you have to have faith to pray? No, it was actually, what is the role of faith in prayer? I thought of my whole "putting it out there" by saying out loud, "I want to climb Mt. Kilimanjaro," and then it happened so much more quickly than I'd expected. Like a prayer answered.

According to Wilson, you don't have to have faith to pray. It goes like this—you make the request and either you get a yes or a no; it's accepted or rejected, or you're asked to wait. And that is of course in the philosophical sense. Those are God's three responses according to Wilson. Yes, no, wait.

And the other thing is, you make the request, you get the response, and then, you have the experience. Beyond that, the next step is for you to evaluate it and determine what to do. I posed the question of my putting it out there that I wanted to climb Mt. Kilimanjaro and now it's here and I still can't believe it. I asked about evaluating it and what does that mean? And Wilson said, "The Big Boss is using you in ways that you don't even know." I asked about how I could extend my lessons, so

93

what are my lessons, and how will I extend them when I go back. That, of course, is the question. And he said, "Don't worry about it. Asking the questions now is too soon. The answers will come. When you get home, there will be an entirely different challenge and you don't even know what it is yet." And I think that's probably very, very true. It was an interesting and thought-provoking conversation.

Although it made me sad to think about what challenges were ahead at home, it was, nonetheless a good conversation and a good evening, dining in the mess tent with the guys. We are the only ones here at camp. I think we'll see other people at lunch time making their way through, but I suspect that we will once again be the only ones here tomorrow night as well. It is peaceful here.

This particular conversation was frustrating and incredibly sad for me because I didn't want to know what any God would say to my question. I already knew the answer: she has a brain tumor and will die. And there wasn't anything I could do to affect that outcome, no matter what questions I asked of whom. Surgeries and treatment had given her more time, but was it worth the suffering she endured?

I knew that when I got home, I would have to learn how to live without her. I was incredibly sad, because I believed that the one to whom it mattered most was me. So much was unresolved: Why did she leave us? Were we bad? My adult mind knew that she did the best that she could, that we weren't bad. My rational mind understood and believed what she'd told us: that she'd made the decision because she thought our father would provide a better life for us. He was a nuclear engineer, she worked for Bell Telephone. We grew up in nice house and had a good primary education; she was right.

But the child within me still wore the scars that hadn't healed, and time was running out. My mother had enough burdens to deal with; she didn't need my unresolved issues added to them. I knew months ago that I had to heal my own hurt; it was the only way. And that's a lonely place to be.

*　　*　　*

In that last recording there was a lot of sniffling, and there were tears. My emotions were raw. I think the time away from home was starting to show. Sending post cards in the afternoon had me thinking of the people I love back home.

I learned from Honest that the men were missing their families too. In the mess tent with all the porters, I noticed Goddy, the wonderful sous chef, looking away and into the distance. I asked Honest if Goddy was okay. Honest told me that Goddy is the father of two little boys, and that he was probably thinking about them in that moment and missing home.

Honest translated my question and there were nods from the others seated around the tent; they were missing home too. I've learned from my time in Africa that family is an incredible source of pride, for both men and women. The depth of feeling these men have for their families was good company; I wasn't alone in missing mine. In that moment I formed a wish for these men: for a happy reunion with their wives and children soon after. I tucked it away, to be shared at the final party.

I remember being incredibly moved by the conversation we had in the mess tent that night and perplexed by how deeply it touched me. I also remember that I didn't care if I cried or not— it was therapeutic to cry in my tent and to indulge in missing home.

*　　*　　*

I love to cook and eat, and find sharing a meal with others to be one of the most enjoyable ways to spend time. No surprise then, that I was curious about the happenings in the mess tent.

At home, I have a typically western diet of meat, chicken, fish, vegetables, dairy, not enough fruit and too much bread. I also have my junk food binges. Curiously, my appetite shifted, noticeably, while I was in Africa. From the first day in Burundi and all throughout the trip, I was enamored of and craving vegetables. I even wondered if I was becoming a vegetarian.

[From my recording] *The crew in the kitchen is top-notch; I don't know how they get done what they get done. They serve these delicious meals, rich soups all prepared from scratch, vegetables all cut up into tiny little pieces and cooked up. Pumpkin soup, zucchini soup, vegetable soup and everything is sweetened with sweet potatoes that are white, unlike what I'm familiar with—the yellow/orange sweet potato at home. These are so sweet when you bite into them. Last night we had a sauce of tomatoes and green peppers over pasta with little green vegetables and some olive oil. But we always start out with a soup. On the mountain, after a long day's walk, let me just tell you: this is food to satisfy the soul.*

Meals are beautifully done and delicious. The fruits and vegetables are cut into little flowers like they have a Japanese ginsu knife to make them; Godlisten—Goddy for short—does this; he is the sous-chef. Goddy is very handy with the knife, creating beautiful plates for each meal.

Also in the kitchen, the mess tent, they have two gas tanks, similar to what you'd have on a gas grill but smaller, and they carry them up. They have a metal tray on top of each, onto which they set pots, which are all aluminum. Light weight is important since they're carrying all of the equipment on their backs and heads. The handles on the pots are aluminum too and they get so hot, yet the chefs lift them up with one towel and they clean the lids as they go.

All the food is washed in water that's been treated with chlorine tablets. Because it's organic, all of the food is carefully cleaned to take off the dirt. They even make sure that the containers are okay. All of this is important for the good health of someone like me whose digestive system isn't used to the bacteria in this environment. They take very good care cleaning all of the food and also all of the utensils that are used—they use the same chlorine-treated water to clean all of the utensils, pot and pans and dishes.

On water, all of the water must be carried up from the streams. Each time we get into camp one or two of the men walk to the nearest stream, then they carry water back up to camp in huge industrial buckets that double as chairs for the men when we're sitting around in the mess tent. The mess tent is where they sit and do their work, in very little light, with their cutting boards on their laps.

Last night Frederick, who is also a chef, cleaned a huge bag of rice for the men, sifting through several platters-full, flicking out the pieces that weren't good enough. He did this in very low light, sitting by the door to use the remaining glow from the end of the day to see what he was doing. They take as much care with the food for the men as for me and this is something that continually impresses me.

As the men ate the rice, I asked about the change-up from their regular menu. They explained it's because today is not a pack-and-carry day for them; I interpreted this to mean that their energy needs are different because today everyone hangs out at camp at Lava Tower. The plan is that we will get up very early tomorrow for an acclimatization climb up to the base of the western breach, which will be our summit approach the following day, and then return to this camp.

Usually the men are eating porridge made from rustic maize flour, rough with pieces of whole corn kernels, and some white raisins. It's good. I've had some in the mornings and it's filling. Solid energy for long walks carrying a lot, and they do: 20 kilograms each, piled on heads, piled on backs; it's unbelievable how much they carry.

They also make ugali, which is a dough-like mixture they form into a small meatball shape, then they eat it with vegetables and fruits and greens. This is appetizingly good-looking; I was jealous watching them rip up and shred gorgeous dark leafy *greens, cook them down, and then eat them with the ugali; I'm sure it was delicious!*

*　　*　　*

On the second afternoon at Lava Tower Camp, Wilson, Honest and I returned from the morning acclimatization hike to Arrow Glacier Camp. We had taken the old route. Now, back at camp where the men were lying out in the sun, I joined them. We were all sitting on a big tarp. They were stretched out and enjoying the sunshine, the depth and rhythm of their Swahili conversation was pleasant and relaxed. The sunshine was uplifting and we all had our faces tilted up toward it on this late afternoon. I had my recorder and, finding a remote corner in the front of the tarp, I recorded some thoughts on the day.

[From my recording] *So the theme for today is humility. We took a walk on the way to Arrow Glacier Camp and it was steep and rocky with a lot of scree[15], and I thought it had been easy up until now, and it had been, but today was scary, and tough, and my muscles were talking back. This is reminding me that the toughest part is yet to come and it will take nerve, and it will take strength, and it will take following Wilson's footsteps—literally— and allowing others to help me, which is not an easy lesson.*

It's a beautiful day, a nice afternoon. It's just past 3 p.m. and there's a whole bunch of people over at Lava Rock. A huge group, screaming back and forth to each other, sounds like more American students.

This morning we saw beautiful springs with patches that froze overnight because it was so cold. They are lovely springs; this is

---

[15] Scree is loose debris of rocks, fallen and crumbled, on the slope of a mountain, steep incline or cliff. According to The American Heritage Dictionary it is probably from the Old Norse word skridha meaning landslide or to slide.

where the men go to get the water we need. Yesterday I had a chance to wash my hair and today I had a chance to rinse out the rest of the soap. After I complained about the feel of it thanks to my lame rinse, they said "Go ahead, use the water!" So I did. And it feels good to let it dry in the sun.

I asked a nice man named Charlie from Minnesota to come over to take a picture of all of us. But we are missing two of the men, who went off to Millennium Camp early this morning. We're paring down what we have and what we'll bring to the summit because we don't need everything and it's crazy to carry everything up, like the dining table! I've been saying that it's okay for me to sit on a rock and have my meal, and I may get my wish because we're letting the dining room table go and keeping just the minimum, just what we need.

The Team at Lava Tower Camp

Today we are a second day at Lava Tower Camp. Tomorrow we will be at Arrow Glacier and we'll explore the area there more fully. And then the next day is when we get up at 5 a.m. and go up the Western Breach. I'd be lying if I told you I wasn't intimidated by it—I am. After today's experience on the field of loose, tumbled rocks, I think it's, well, it's steep as hell with scree and boulders, so this is the real challenge about to happen and tomorrow I'll work hard and breathe and drink a lot of water, because I genuinely want to make it. That's the big climb.

It's funny—they say "The work is off the mountain," yet in this case, the work is not even hitting that final point at the summit, although I know that that will be work, but it's the western breach that's the scary part for me. Wilson says, "When you tell people you took this route, they will respect you," and I believe him because it's an intimidating route. So that's the plan.

Some notes before I forget: Bring lots of warm clothes. Definitely I didn't bring enough warm clothing. I have enough, but I could have used more. And sunscreen – you need it, you need it, you need it. You are 180 miles from the equator so it's close to the sun.

*   *   *

[From a later recording] *Today's theme is about facing your fears and overcoming them. It's near the end of the day, about 5:00 p.m. And we're still at Lava Tower. Over the past two hours I've heard two sounds of what I'm sure are calving glaciers[16] and think to myself, "Will we be walking under them? Will the path*

---

[16] Glaciers make a tremendous crackling-boom sound when their outer edges fall away in big slices; that falling away is known as 'calving.' Icebergs are pieces of glacier that have fallen away, calved and thus been born into the sea. I've witnessed calving glaciers and avalanches and know that even from a short distance, the piercing crack of sound is delayed; it reaches the ear only *after* the ice has broken away.

still be there?" Who knows? So today's theme: facing and overcoming your fears.

From a later recording, before bed: Tonight I had dinner early but that gave me the chance to stay awhile in the tent with the guys, to drink a lot of tea and listen to good conversation. I'm able to stay warm when I'm in the mess tent because it's the warmest tent. Of course now that we've let the porter tent go, it's the only tent in which we all fit. I had ugali with greens and they taught me how to roll it in my hands like a small meatball, then how to make an indentation in it so that you can scoop some greens in there and it was very filling and very good. It was awfully nice of them to share their meal with me. So it was a good evening and now I'm ready to turn in for the night. And it's incredibly cold! Good night!

What I remember most about this particular day, is this: the day hike was intimidating. I walked across an avalanche bridge of rock—scrambled and crumbling—and I thought, at any moment this could slide and me with it. It reminded me of a hike in Norway.

On the Norway hike, we started in the morning, passed by an awe-inspiring, expansive glacier, and then by late afternoon we were very near the pinnacle of our climb, which afforded a gorgeous view straight down a fiord. We crossed over natural snow and ice bridges and could hear the water rushing far beneath and below. Nearing the top, literally just two long, tall steps and a hand-pull-yourself-up away, I stepped through a lip of snow next to a rock. The sun had been beating on the dark rock during the day, warming it and softening the snow around it. I stepped through and quickly—miraculously—found a hold with my hands, and then pulled my leg out. Looking down to where my leg had been, in up to the thigh, I stared down into black nothingness. Instinct told me to focus on pulling myself up onto the rock and onto the flat, solid ground immediately above it where my family stood. It wasn't until I reached the top that I thought about how close a call that had just been.

Back on the avalanche slide, on the way to Arrow Glacier Camp: this was the "old route" to the western breach of the crater because an avalanche had wiped out the camp, leaving the partially buried remnants of out-houses exposed and tilting. The same avalanche that we were now walking over did this.

I stepped on a round stone and heard other stones beneath it take what sounded like a very looonnnggg fall. I didn't have to cognitively remember the close call in Norway because my body recalled on its own, rushing adrenaline to the rest of me so I could walk carefully, with restraint, to safety. My heart was pounding and I tried to remember to breathe regularly. The sound of those rocks falling, far away beneath my feet, shook my confidence. *Welcome back, my fear.* I hate when that happens.

Later, Wilson told me that he'd finally spotted my weakness, that he watches all of his clients to find out what might trip them up and this was my trip wire—crossing over loose rock. Feeling at first like I'd been found out, I quickly rationalized that I was in expert hands and appreciated that Wilson knew. Now that he knew, I would work to prove it wrong (twisted, I know, but it helped).

I also acknowledged to myself that *despite my fear, I had kept going*, breathing and stepping carefully. I kept moving forward. I didn't freeze like I'd done before in Vermont when my son Chip had to hold both of my hands and talk me through a short leap over a two-foot wide drop-to-nothing chasm, or in Zermatt when I had an emotional meltdown crossing an open metal bridge high up on the Matterhorn and had to turn back.

No, not this day and not this place; I'd been allowed to go this far and I knew I was supposed to keep going. And so I did—because we had to cross over it again to return to Lava Tower Camp, and the next day we followed the very same route to get to the new Arrow Glacier Camp.

Face your fears. Because if you don't, they'll just keep coming back until you acknowledge them and learn how to live *with* them.

DAY 9

"Travel is more than the seeing of sights; it is a change that goes on, deep and permanent, in the ideas of living." – Miriam Beard

[From my SENE itinerary] *Lava Tower Camp (15,230') to Arrow Glacier Camp (15,980'), 1.7 miles.* *"We climb higher up the mountain from the west, moving polé-polé (meaning "slowly" in Kiswahili[17]) to let our bodies rest from the exertion and to acclimate to the thin air. Total hiking time is only about 2 hours. With clear weather you will have a closeup view of the Western Breach, through which we will ascend to the crater tomorrow."*

[From my recording] *Ok, it's Saturday morning. I know this because I confirmed last evening that it was Friday, otherwise I wasn't sure what day of the week it is. So it's Saturday morning, we're leaving Lava Camp and heading over to Arrow Glacier, where we'll take an afternoon walk along the path that we will ultimately take to the base of the glacier. Maybe today's theme is "humble and smart." Humble and smart. We'll develop that more as we go through the day.*

A couple of thoughts: my blood numbers continue to look very good and I'm incredibly pleased with this. All I have to do is take a couple of deep breaths, and they go up, which is good. I started off in the high 90s and am now in the high 80s; I'd like to keep it there. If you get to 60, they make you turn back. Is it the Diamox? Is it just me? I don't know, but if there is something available to help me, I'm going to say "Hakuna matata," No problems. Hakuna matata. No worries. And now it's time to get dressed and get ready for the day.

---

[17] Kiswahili and Swahili both represent the language spoken in East Africa. The difference is that Kiswahili refers only to the language, whereas Swahili refers to both the language and the culture of the East African countries where it is a common language (Tanzania, Burundi, Kenya, DRC, Rwanda, Uganda, Mozambique and South Sudan).

Several more of the team was preparing to leave us at this point; they'd be heading down to re-stock our provisions and set up our tents at Millennium Camp where we'd meet up again. I'd been rationing my Costco trail mix—a delicious blend of nuts, dried fruits and M&Ms—to be sure there was enough for everyone. The little bags were puffed up by the elevation. I handed each man a puffy snack pillow, and gave each one a Namaste bow to express my thanks for all that they'd done up until now. Honest translated that I wished them all a safe and good journey.

*   *   *

[From my recording] *Saturday again and we are walking over to Arrow Glacier Camp. Along the way I'm reminded of some of the notes I wanted to take.*

In the glacier area there are different kinds of rocks and it's amazing that they all come from the same place. The colors range from deep glacial blue green to this rich red and grey. Many of the grey rocks are flecked—in fact, many of the russet are flecked as well, which I've learned from reading and from my guides, is unique to Mt. Kilimanjaro. These rocks have rhombus crystals on the inside that glint in the sunlight and catch the eyes. They are absolutely stunning.

I've also noticed this morning the lichen—it's incredible—it's reminding me of the old-time colors of the Miami Dolphins, bright orange and turquoise blue. I'm staring at some right now that is yellow-green. I haven't seen so much orange lichen on any other mountain—another thing that makes this place unique.

At one point on the trail I found a perfectly-formed, cleanly-extracted specimen of the rhombic crystals that live in these grand rocks; to me, it was like finding treasure. I held it, delighted by the intellectual find, since I'd only read about it in Wilson's guidebook, and for days now, I'd been winked at by the sliced off tops of these crystals embedded in the larger lava rock.

I turned it around in my hand to examine every bit of its curious form, and then returned it to the dusty trail.

The technical name for the larger rock is rhomb porphyry lava, and it's distinctive because of its embedded crystals, like the one I'd just held in my hand. They are, lengthwise, rhombic-shaped, with a diamond-shaped top where they'd been horizontally sliced. I tried to find an illustration but there's none to be found—I'm sorry I didn't take a picture so you could see it too. According to Wilson's "guide's guide" of the mountain, this is actually another form of lava that poured from these volcanos 360,000 years ago, and it is unique to the Mt. Kilimanjaro area, found on this mountain as well as neighboring Mt. Meru. To me, it was fascinating.

Wilson wanted to listen to his radio, which was interesting at first, but the short program repeated over and over again and quickly became annoying. "Do you mind if I listen to my radio?" he asked. The first time he asked I nodded okay. I remember thinking at the time that it was Sunday, the Sabbath and probably an important day for Wilson, so I went with the flow.

But when he asked again I told him I'd prefer not to have the radio on. I was surprised to see Honest nodding to me in agreement; I guess he preferred the quiet of the trails too. The rest of the day's walk, whichever day of the week it was, was blissfully peaceful.

*   *   *

[From my recording] *Well, just finished lunch at Arrow base camp. The original idea was to take a walk over to see the bottom of the glacier for pictures but we are socked in with clouds. Fluffy gorgeous clouds that break every once in a while, providing a small opening through which you can tell it's sunny below. It has started to sleet so we've decided not to do the scenic hike. I've been informed by my guides that it's not for acclimatization—that was yesterday—it's actually for pictures. So, that's okay, it works out okay that we're not going all the way over there in this weather. The trick now is to conserve energy and be nice and strong for tomorrow, early morning, when we climb the western breach.*

We tried to call Alan again on cell today. Even though it's Saturday and I'm not sure where in the world he is, we did try to call. My cell phone battery is completely dead; I thought maybe it was cold but it's completely dead. Wilson offered his phone again but we couldn't get it to dial; there was a message about it being an invalid number. Even with the extra zero that worked at Mbahe, the call didn't go through.

But I know that the guides are phoning in to the office. I wish I could say to Alan, "if you need to find out how I'm doing, you can. You can find out through the office." I did try to call from Shira 2 Camp, but I was not able to get through. I tried Karen, I tried Alan, but I wasn't able to get through, it just wouldn't work. My uber-reliable Burundian phone with the Airtel card purchased in Nairobi, guaranteed to work in Tanzania, DOES work in Tanzania but apparently not on Kilimanjaro. I look forward to recharging it when I get back to Mbahe Farm and to calling you then. Bye for now.

*   *   *

Arrow Glacier Camp was cold with whipping winds. It was a long afternoon of sitting in my tent to keep warm, reading Stedman, and reading the book Wilson loaned me about the flora and fauna on the mountain. I could hear the sleet hitting the outer shell of my tent.

Before I left home, I made a conscious decision not to bring a novel or music with me on this trip. It was and remained my 'purist' intention: to be present for all the sights and sounds, to let the experience itself be the story. This allowed me to spend time simply appreciating the sights, sounds, smells, the feel of the wind, the sun glinting on the rock, and of course, the flora and fauna—which at this altitude are strictly lichen. It also allowed more time alone with my thoughts.

There was an astonishing amount of trash at Arrow Glacier Camp. It was the most littered camping area I'd seen thus far, which made me sad.

Seeing so much trash in this beautiful place, combined with feeling anxious about the next day's climb, triggered the head games my mind sometimes plays about being "less-than" and wondering why. Fear had left the door open and self-doubt crept in. During some of my darker moments in life, I have wondered, what it was about me that made me disposable to my parents? Why was it so easy for them to discard me, like some of the trash I was staring at? I normally don't stay with that thought for long, because I realize it's counter-productive and, intellectually, I know that they regretted their choices.

I remind myself that it's part of being human to sometimes make choices we regret. I know I have. It pains me deeply to recall those times when I've been mean, dismissive, rude, inconsiderate or hurtful to another human being, or when I've let them down.

My mother and I have had a good relationship, especially after I'd moved back to the Philadelphia area as an adult and saw her more frequently. During one of our phone calls a few years ago, she asked me to forgive her—out of the blue. I knew what she meant, but the request was so unexpected I found myself speechless, which is unusual for me. I knew in my head that the proper response was to use the same word—forgive—but the sensation in my gut held me back. It didn't seem the right thing to say. Like trying to cross a deep chasm, I was immobilized and could not take a step.

After a pause, I reassured her that I knew she'd done the best she could. But I could not, at that time, say "Oh, it's okay." I could not yet say the words, "I forgive you." It was beyond my reach, yet it shouldn't have been, and I've been carrying the shame of that conversation for a long time. In that moment, I began to understand that what I'd been carrying was her burden too, because I was a reminder of choices she'd regretted. We left it there, and I've always wondered if it was enough.

Although my mother and I made peace with each other, in a way, in that moment, I never have been able to understand why my father didn't speak to me for ten years after I graduated from high school. I believe I've moved past it though, made peace with it, and it's no longer a burden; it's just an anomaly.

Now, at this moment, thousands of miles from home, where my mother was dying, these memories of my fractured childhood emerged. This was the realm of thoughts I'd hoped to escape by coming to Africa. But here they were, in the tent with me. Even though I knew my parents' divorce wasn't about me, and even though, intellectually, I understood why there needed to be a clear chain of command in charge of her care, it still made me incredibly sad. Being tossed aside during this difficult time had re-opened old emotional wounds, the kind that didn't respond to rationalization.

I realized, on the mountain, that there are no do-overs with family, just forgiveness, and that most of the time I am emotionally clear enough to remember that this is a choice.

Just outside, towering over my little tent at Arrow Glacier Camp, were huge craggy rock formations. "They're old," Wilson told me, and I wondered secretly if they'd crumble onto my tent and crush me. I decided it was better not to think about it, trusting the team would not put my tent up here and out of the way if it weren't safe. In fact, I think they did it to give me a wind barrier.

If I had it to do again, I'd bring bags to pick up trash at Arrow Glacier camp. And I'd endeavor to walk over to see Arrow Glacier before carrying that trash down and out of this incredible park.

*   *   *

This part of the journey made me nervous. The trekking had been relatively easy up to this point, but the breach is an intimidating rock face and from my low vantage point it was towering above me, several thousand feet of big boulder: a tall rocky wall sticking straight up. All that I'd read indicated BIG RESPECT was appropriate and in order. I worried for the safety of the men, maybe to avoid worrying about my own.

After dinner on the evening before we "attacked the Breach," as they say in climbing parlance, I must have been looking fearful because Honest gave me strong advice. He pointed to his thighs and said, "Deb, I know you are very strong here. What I need is for you to be strong HERE," as he tapped his head. I nodded yes, and told him I'd work on it that evening.

I slept with a field of avalanche scree on one side of my tent, just beneath a lumbering wall of well-worn rock that looked about ready to crumble, on the other side. It was windy and cold and forbidding (or was that just me?).

*   *   *

When I was writing this chapter, I remembered a passage from Mark Nepo.

> "Wherever we stop is the summit . . . I was overcome with the sudden truth that I could go no farther, and that I had no need to go any farther."[18]

To me, this comparison of climbing and fear is similar to SENE's O_2 rule: if you hit 60, you've reached your summit; congratulations and we're escorting you down.

---

[18] Material excerpted from the book THE BOOK OF AWAKENING ©2000 Mark Nepo with permission from Red Wheel/Weiser, LLC Newburyport, MA and San Francisco, CA www.redwheelweiser.com.

I know what it's like to hit the summit prematurely.

It had happened to me on the Matterhorn, where I was almost paralyzed with fear on an incredibly dangerous path of open metal, twisted and bent with pieces missing, taken out by falling rock. Was I hyperventilating? Probably. I was gripping the rail for dear life and though I'd made it almost to the other end, I reached a point where I absolutely could not take one more step forward. I knew with every frightened cell in my body that I had to turn back.

Crouched low and with a death grip on the rail, I made it back to the other side, returning to where I'd started. A couple offered their hands to help me off the twisted metal ledge. I started crying in a release of emotion, at the kindness of the couple, and that I'd landed on terra firma. I had been terrified, and I was incredibly relieved to have survived.

The woman, witnessing my emotional release said to her husband, "See, I told you this is scary!" and then she told me the story of her father who, on a visit from Germany just a week before, had fallen through one of the bent and broken pieces of the open metal scaffold that I'd just crossed, twice. He was saved by his rucksack, which caught on a rung as he fell through, preventing him from falling hundreds of feet to what surely would have been his death. He dislocated his shoulder, but he survived.

I did not want to have another Matterhorn moment of emotional hijacking here. On Kilimanjaro, I wanted to be brave and clear of mind. I wanted to make it to the top, to whatever was above and beyond the Western Breach. I wasn't even thinking about the summit here, just the Breach, only the Breach. I wanted to feel the fear and move forward despite it, not to be paralyzed and hyperventilating, stopped in my tracks by it. I wanted to be able to keep moving forward, I wanted life to keep moving forward. I could not control anything to do with my mother's dying, her requests, wishes or choices. But I could make it through this challenge and bring home within me the confidence of one who has seen from the summit; I wanted to bring that home in my heart.   But on the scale of fear and bravery, each weighed equally in my mind that day at Arrow Glacier Camp.

Humility also loomed large for me on Mt. Kilimanjaro that day and despite my fear, I knew in the depths of my soul that I would not turn back. I could not turn back. Since leaving a stifling job in 2007, my first day of freedom on Labor Day (yes, this was definitely cosmic humor), I now know and believe that I have options. In fact, making the decision to leave that job I felt stuck in is when I first discovered there were, actually, other options. Before then, I could see only "stuck."

I can't recall where I first heard this unforgettable acronym but I love it.   I refer to it, and refer others to it, often: Remember, YAHOO (you always have other options) and never forget it.

The option was always there to turn back on Mt. Kilimanjaro, but it never occurred to me to pursue it because I'd come so far and knew the best was yet to come. This was no Matterhorn, this was Kilimanjaro and she'd welcomed me with that magical sunrise a few days before; I knew it would be okay since, after all, "all things happen for good."

DAY 10

[From my SENE Itinerary] *Arrow Glacier Camp (15,980') to Crater Camp (18,800'), 1.6 miles. "We will rise well before sunrise, eat a hearty breakfast, strap on SENE-provided helmets, and begin our ascent of the Western Breach by 5:00 a.m. The climb is a steep and invigorating challenge, but with several days on the mountain behind you, you will be physically and mentally sharp for the ascent. The trail has sections of scree and sections requiring scrambling over boulders. As you reach the lip of the crater your elation will be second only to that when summiting Uhuru Peak tomorrow. The wide crater floor is a magnificent arctic moonscape; our camp is set in soft sand near the indigo streaked Furtwangler Glacier."*

Looking again at my SENE itinerary, I can't believe this was only 1.6 miles. Yeah, 1.6 miles **straight up!**

Everything I'd read stressed the importance of crossing under Arrow Glacier as early as possible, before the sun hit and loosened up the rocks. I was anxious to get going and concerned for the safety of us all. I don't remember hesitating to get up and out of my sleeping bag; it was a very serious morning for me. Wilson and Honest waited for me below and I can't remember now eating breakfast though I'm sure we did. I just wanted to get going while it was early and before the sun came up.

This part of the trek has some legal requirements. Climbers are required to wear a helmet to protect them from avalanche or their own falling, which is silly when you think about tons of rock falling on you—a helmet won't do much to save you from that. But it's the law and so Honest put my helmet on.

I was grateful for the help because I could not believe how cold my hands were. I told the guides that I believed I'd made a serious error here—that my hands were extremely cold. They rubbed my hands to warm them, which made me feel silly. I had two pair of gloves on but they were both too big for me. They were Alan's gloves. Why didn't I listen to Matt Friedman, the

Kili-climber who'd come to dinner in my home, when he told me to bring the warmest gloves I own? None of mine would have been enough. Why didn't I buy new ones? Ugh.

I rallied quickly, realizing that movement would be the best remedy for cold hands. I knew that this would not stop me. It was time to go.

For the past two nights the men had kept two of my water bottles in their tent after they'd frozen overnight in mine. I did all that I could to keep the CamelBak warm; I blew into the tube to clear the water from it, as instructed, but it froze up anyway.

Hakuna Matata, no worries. I knew I could drink from the water bottles for the first part of the trek. Honest played his water bottle tune every once in a while along the way. A client had given him the silliest water bottle with Hoops and YoYo singing "Drink, drink, drink your water," which I obligingly did. On this part of the trek Honest pulled the water bottle from my pack for me each time. Of course I'd rather have done it on my own, but it was steep on the Breach, and I was humbled into accepting his assistance. I even let him hold onto my walking poles when I scrambled up the rocks. For drinking water, it sure was easier with the CamelBak, which did defrost when the sun came around, so eventually no hands, no help needed.

We made our way across the fallen rock slide and it was steep. We stepped gently over small frozen streams of water. Looking backward and down, we waved to the men as they broke down camp. Soon they would pass us, as they always did.

Then we were into big rock territory. My breathing was labored but we took it polé-polé and did just fine. Sometimes I used my walking sticks, sometimes I didn't. Wilson was attentive to my steps and Honest to my water and poles—I felt babied, frankly; all this being taken care of does not fit with my independent, DIY (*Do It Yourself*) style.

Wilson instructed me to follow his steps exactly but his legs are shorter than mine and I was more comfortable making my own steps, stretching arms and legs up and over, using my hands to

114

grab onto the next rocks up. Despite the pounding headache that was developing, I have to tell you that I WAS LOVING THIS ROCK SCRAMBLE! I thought several times about Chip and Mike and how much FUN they would have doing this.

We took brief rest stops along the way for water and to catch our breath. Honest was just fine but Wilson had been sucking up trail dust and it was evident in his raspy respiration. Wilson said to me at one point, "I can hear you breathing," and I assured him that I was doing fine; I could hear my breathing too. My lungs were congested but it was to me a curiosity much more than a concern.

I allowed myself to very briefly look straight down . . .

I allowed myself to look straight up . . .

But only when we were seated or stopped.

I refrained from looking up or down while we were on the move because frankly, it was one seriously steep wall of boulders. Looking anywhere other than in my immediate proximity, in any direction, even when seated, helped me understand what vertigo must feel like. I thought it best just to focus on what was near and next.

There's a picture of Wilson and me at a rest along the way and though the incline is visible, I don't think it adequately captures the feel of the pitch.

Wilson and me

If I were to do it again, I'd push myself to appreciate this place more; I'd risk the panic and feel the fear of looking down and up more frequently.

Before I knew it, we were crowning the Western Breach and stepping into the crater.

I couldn't believe what I saw: HUGE glaciers, directly in front of me!!! I ran over to see them, leaving Wilson and Honest to wonder, as they told me a few minutes later, "Who is this woman with all the energy at 18,800 feet after a seven hour climb?!" In that moment I was thinking about how incredibly beautiful it was.

We made our way to the right, to the camp, and my energy sapped quickly. The headache was a raging one and I knew it was from the altitude. Fortunately it was tea time—with popcorn, my favorite—and then I had about an hour to take a nap in my tent. I took some ibuprofen for the headache and tried to get some rest but the pounding in my head was unrelenting.

I remember quite clearly that there were people walking by my tent, and they were talking loudly. I thought they were so rude. It sounded like they were booming their voices, almost shouting their conversation. It sounded like they were right next to my tent, even though I understood that they were walking by and would not have passed so closely to another person's tent. Who were these rude people? At the same time I thought they were rude, I knew it was the headache. My head hurt so much that I couldn't even make a sound to shush them. I tried, it hurt, I stopped. Rest wasn't coming. Then it was time for the special hike I'd requested, over to the interior of the crater.

There is narrated footage of the crater on video, which I share with you at www.HerSoloSummit.com.

We walked on frozen patches and through loose, soft, dark gray sand, the fine kind you'd find on a beach. It wasn't easy to walk on and required more energy expenditure than walking on flat, firm ground. The sun was bright up there and with zero clouds that high up—we were at 18,800 feet (!!!)—I was grateful for my polarized sunglasses and baseball cap.

We walked over to the Reusch Crater, which required slightly more elevation; this would be our acclimatization hike today. Walk high, sleep low; that's the recipe for acclimatization.

The Reusch Crater was other-worldly. Clearly the cone of a volcano, there were visible layers to the surface of the inside walls that led below to where smaller craters were visible. I could smell the sulfur and see the warm wispy clouds of it down below where the ground is supposedly warm to the touch.

I contemplated the walk down there, to feel the warm ground—I had wanted to do that when I was planning, and had even made a special request for it. But, my head hurt a lot, and I knew that I didn't have the energy to walk down into the pit and out again, which would have taken a couple of hours. I thought about it several times as I looked over the edge, and realized I could live with taking Stedman's word for it—that the ground was warm to the touch down there. I reasoned that being able to see it would be enough for me. I also considered that, with this headache, the sulfur might just do me in if I got much closer to it.

Despite the headache, there was something about that afternoon—perhaps it was seeing our long shadows reflecting on the crater's edge and realizing the day was coming to an end—that inspired nostalgia and made me want to stay a while longer, even though I knew it was time to go. I had a recollected sense of late Fall evenings when, as kids, we wouldn't want to come in for dinner because we were in the middle of kickball or tag or some other game outside. We wandered around above the crater, took some pictures and video, but the shadows were getting longer still, and we all agreed it was best to head back to Camp. I was looking forward to salty, warm soup.

I ate in the mess tent with our considerably smaller team. The headache remained and my appetite was less than what it normally was. The soup we had that night was different; I asked and learned it had come from a dehydrated packet, so the soup wasn't what it normally was either. But it was salty and warm, and once again, I didn't have to prepare or clean up—I only had to sit there to be served—who can complain about that?

Though I did try to eat, I wasn't hungry for much more beyond the soup. Honest commented, "You're not eating," with a look that indicated concern, since loss of appetite is a sign of AMS. I reminded him that we'd had tea just a few hours ago and told him that aside from the headache, I felt good, just not hungry.

Being so very proud of myself for what I'd accomplished that day, I turned in early for a well-deserved sleep. I faced a big fear and overcame it. On that day, I climbed the Western Breach and on that night, I would be sleeping in the crater of a volcano on the roof of Africa. To me, this was the summit I had hoped for.

*   *   *

Listening to my recordings as I was writing this book, I wondered if sounds travel differently at higher altitude; the air is thinner and the pressure lower, after all. What is the combined effect? Could this also explain the extra volume from those people who walked by my tent? Or, what is the altitudinal impact on hearing? Or was it just a bad headache?

On the recordings made in the crater, my breathing was heavy and somewhat labored (altitude); my speech was slow (cold); and I heard scratchy noises, even some whispering to myself. I found it interesting how QUIET this recording was, since the other recordings had wind and/or the voices of the crew in the background, even when I recorded in my tent. Here, though, all of my movements—breathing, zipping bags, moving around—were amplified.

My research confounded me, so I posed the questions to Don Lockwood, retired rocket scientist and former professor at California Polytechnic Institute, and learned a few key facts that helped me understand:

First, "The speed of sound decreases with temperature and altitude, which will change the pitch of various sounds. The change in Mach number [how fast sound moves] is significant between sea level and say 18,000 feet. The lack of background noise could make your own hearing more sensitive to the sounds that were present; for example, it's easier to hear a voice in a quiet room rather than in a crowded one."

According to my Uncle Don, "The recording issue presents a different problem. Some recording equipment has an AGC (automatic gain control) and noise suppression built into the software. The thinner air at altitude could reduce the impact of the air molecules on the recording membrane, and that might fool the AGC and noise suppression into thinking the sound was at a lower level than it actually was."

The tape recorder—I hadn't even considered that option.

*   *   *

[From my recording] *So, there are certain parts of the western breach that you want to tackle when it's very cold, when loose ground is held together by ice. Crossing that part took us a couple of hours and then even after the sun came up, we were still on the dark side of the mountain. The sun was coming up over the peaks, which were above us. And so we could see the sunlight on the clouds, but we were still in the shade.*

This was SO EXCITING, quite long, literally seven hours long, very steep, an uber-cool rock scramble. With scree. Chip and Mike would love this. It was thrilling, and it was a flawless day.

The summit is 90 minutes above my head, literally, and quite frankly getting there feels like a piece of cake to me, because the western breach was the indisputably big challenge and I did it!

Dark side of the moon is the theme for today. We started the climb, it wasn't dark, we didn't need our headlamps, we left early, at 6 or 6:15 am. Then we got to the crater rim, breached the crater rim via the western breach about seven hours later and it was like being on the moon, on the surface of the moon.

We came to camp. These porters are unbelievable—how they carry everything up, and I'm sucking wind. Actually, I've been sucking a lot of dust from the trail, so I have a deep lung cough. We don't think it's AMS, we think it's definitely from the trail. But my O_2 numbers are getting into the worrisome range, for me, since once you hit 60 they declare that you have summited and then you are invited to go back down. Well we're 90 minutes from summit and tonight's number is about 69, maybe lower. So I need to drink more water, I'm taking the Diamox which I think makes a big difference, but I've got a killer headache. It started at maybe about 17.5K or 18K feet, and it's not responding to ibuprofen. But maybe tonight, with a good night's sleep, that should help. And then tomorrow it's not that much higher, and then we're on our way down. So that's the report. From the moon.

Remembering this day makes my heart sing.

[From my recording, recorded in the evening, in my tent, at Crater Camp] *Some other honorable mentions. Last night I was so cold. I didn't have enough layers. I had one wool layer, top and bottom. So tonight I have lots of layers, including wool underwear, wool pants, double socks, 200 wool + 260 + fleece. I'm not messin' around tonight 'cause it's gonna be cold. Glaciers live in this crater; it's going to be cold. That's it.*

I did fall asleep. And I did have to get up in the middle of the night to visit the bathroom. My hands were shaking so much from the cold that I dropped the entire little roll of TP into the biological toilet.

It was so quiet. As I did every other night, I stood outside and gave myself a hug in an attempt to stay warm. It took effort but I wanted to force myself to stick it out for a few minutes in the freezing cold, just to take mental snapshots of what I saw and heard and felt there.

On this night, I stood outside and looked at the huge glaciers standing guard near our camp, iridescent blue in the moonlight. The moon was just three days beyond full and still very big in the sky. The glaciers were luminous, as though lit from within.

We were high above the clouds, where the air is thin with very little O_2. From an altitude of 18,800 feet the sky looked black and the stars were brilliant, the view of them blocked by nothing man-made. It was still, calm, quiet; there was no sound, not even the wind.

Words cannot capture the depth of feeling associated with those moments, that night. I was in awe. Standing in the crater of an ancient volcano, I thought about how she welcomed me when we first saw each other and on this night, in this other-worldly place, I had a sense that she was sharing the gift of timelessness and peace, with me.

Observe the wonders as they occur around you.
Don't claim them.
Feel the artistry moving through,
and be silent.

-Rumi

DAY 11

[From my recording, in my tent, in the morning at Crater Camp]
The sounds of the glaciers, you can hear them crackling, settling. Contracting is more like it but then, we're lying on the ground floor, so you can FEEL them making noises, which is fascinating to me—they're like a drum beat, a big drum beat.

In the morning I was woken up by a feeling—not an emotion but a vibration. And a sound. It happened again and I tried to wake up, to think about how I'd describe it. It was like a bass drum, I decided, not so much loud as it was deep. I thought to myself, *"I am sleeping in the crater of a volcano, maybe the lava is boiling deep, deep down? I wonder if the volcano is going to erupt?"*

"Boom." Muffled yet powerful, I felt it in my body. *No, silly, it's not the volcano.*

"Boom." *I'm sleeping on a mat, in a tent, on the ground. The sun is rising, and the glaciers are stretching like old men in the morning, making their creaking sounds.*

I sat up and pulled out my tiny, cracked mirror to see what my hair looked like and thought, *thank goodness for hats.* Immediately I noticed that my eyes were puffy. My first thought was that I must be retaining fluid and that was not a good sign since fluid retention, especially in the lungs and around the brain, is another symptom of AMS. But we were almost there and we'd be heading down in just a few hours.

Honest arrived at my tent to take my vitals. He didn't say anything about my puffy eyes, so I didn't either. My blood oxygen registered at 64 on the first try and I wasn't happy with the number; it made me nervous. Although 64 is not 60, I was competing with myself to keep the numbers high and wasn't satisfied with a reading in the low 60s range. Not at all.

We were too close to turn back, and I knew the device could make mistakes. I asked Honest to give me a minute; I'd just woken up after all.

I wasn't in the danger zone yet, but since it had become a personal challenge to me to have good oxygen readings. I wanted another shot at it. I knew I could get a better number. I took a few good, deep breaths, then he took the reading again. It was 68. I was relieved and pleased and maybe Honest was, too.

The sun was gloriously bright that morning in the crater. I can't remember if we ate breakfast or not. I think we may have decided on tea and to then be on our way. From where we camped, we could see the groups of people who'd already made it to the summit, lined up and waiting for their photo ops. Soon, we'd be there too.

After the victory of the Breach yesterday, I was looking forward to reaching the summit, although I must confess, it seemed strangely anti-climactic. I felt peaceful, as if relieved of the weight of my fear. On that day, I was most definitely a lighter presence in the world.

*　　*　　*

"It always seems impossible until it's done." – Nelson Mandela

[From my SENE itinerary] *Crater Camp (18,800') to Uhuru Peak (19,340') to Millennium Camp (12,530'), 5.9 miles. "After an early breakfast we make the final ascent to Uhuru Peak, reaching the 19,340 foot summit of Kilimanjaro by 8 a.m. At this early hour, before the clouds close in, you will have spectacular views of Africa in all directions. After a stay of 20 to 30 minutes with tea, snacks, and plenty of photos, we descend 2 to 3 hours to Barafu Camp for lunch, rest, and to take off extra layers. Continuing downhill 3 to 4 hours to the edge of the Mweka Forest, we reach the final night's camp - 7,000 feet below the summit! Eat, share your experiences of the climb, and sleep soundly. Congratulations, you touched the Roof of Africa!"*

We went polé-polé for about 90 minutes and made it to the top. We walked up on a steep incline that was loose and sandy, so every two steps you'd lose a half step, because it was hard to get a grip. But we kept going. It helped to push a boot toe in and forward, and to use the walking sticks. We had to go slowly. Going slowly worked since, when we didn't go slowly, I became winded. And, as I reassured myself along the way, it's the same for everyone on this part of the trail.

Along the way we were passed by a small group of people who had also camped out in the crater. Though noisy when passing my tent, they had camped a considerable distance from us. This morning they came as if from nowhere, a surprise. I wouldn't find out until almost a year later, when one of them came to my home for dinner, that this was not the group that had camped in the crater; that group had summited long before us. No, this group had begun their traverse much earlier—in the middle of the night—and had passed through to experience the crater before making their way to the summit.

Honest was in the lead and it pains me to admit this, but it was work for me to keep up with his pace. Honest is younger and he was moving faster. I chuckled to myself because in that moment I actually missed Wilson's slow and steady polé-polé pace.

Eventually we made our way to the top, approaching the summit from the opposite direction of almost all the others there. I snapped a photo of an unnamed cairn and wondered if it was marking the trail down and into the crater, or if it was the spot some say is the de facto highest point on the mountain when measured by GPS.

We made our way over to the sign marking the summit and waited as two groups finished their photos. There were four of us: Honest, Wilson and me, and Vernance, who carried the Gamow bag and oxygen all the way to the top, just in case.

The Gamow bag is a pressurized body bag used to treat Altitude Sickness, and it's something else that sets this company apart from others because they insist on its use. Other companies will let you rent one, should you choose to, but SENE teams don't climb without it. If you end up in the Gamow bag, you're being carried down on the "Kilimanjaro Express," and I would not want to be bumped along mountain trails at high speed on one of those, but at least you'd be alive and heading down to feeling better. I'm truly thankful that I didn't need to be escorted down.

Safety and preventing AMS are paramount to SENE. Based on what I've read, I believe they're in the minority of companies who check vitals twice each day; they do this for the whole team as well as their clients, and record it for everyone. I asked Honest if I could have the sheet on which he recorded my vitals and he provided me with a copy of it before I left. It was an interesting souvenir for me, a way to track my progress and to be able to look back at my "Kilimanjaro report card."

In just a few minutes it was our turn at the big sign, where we posed for pictures and enjoyed the view all around the summit. I made some good videos for you to see and hear about the glaciers, and the view from the top. You can see a full 360 panorama in the videos at www.HerSoloSummit.com.

On The Roof

Then it was time to head down.

It's strange to say this, but, to me, the summit felt anti-climactic. The breach, on the other hand, was a formidable accomplishment; although it had intimidated me, I ended up having a lot of fun with.

What would I do if I were not afraid? The answer surprised me.

It still surprises me how much fun I had scrambling on that rock wall. Once I let go of the fear, I felt liberated, free, and I truly enjoyed myself. I think it helped, too, that I was able to make my own moves on those rocks, reaching and pulling myself up to the next one and then the next one. I enjoyed having a chance to improvise and actually make my own way for parts of what I thought would be the worst. And it turned out to be the best.

The next recording was made many hours later, in the early evening of summit day, from Millennium Camp. Listening later to the recording, I noted that my voice was much clearer and stronger now that we'd come back to a lower elevation, then I realized it was actually 12,530 feet and that's very near where I'd previously gotten the "altitude dizzies." I was sounding and feeling strong at an altitude where I used to feel like throwing up—now that's something to celebrate.

[From my recording] *It's the next to last day on the trail, tomorrow is a short walk out to the Mweke gate, where we'll be picked up and brought back to Simon's farm for a party. But today, I'd like to describe.*

We reached the summit, Uhuru Peak, where I left two rocks behind. They are my contribution to the restoration of the summit to its full height.

Uhuru means "Freedom." There is a quote from when Kilimanjaro was dedicated and they put a flame at Uhuru peak. The dedication speech refers to giving hope where there is none and peace in the world, and to me, that is a meaningful sentiment.

> "We, the people of Tanganyika, would like to light a candle and put it on the top of Mount Kilimanjaro which would shine beyond our borders giving hope where there was despair, love where there was hate, and dignity where there was before only humiliation."
>
> -Julius Nyerere, First President of Tanzania, from his 1961 speech "A Candle on Kilmanjaro"

[Continued from my recording] *Walking around up at the peak you see the glaciers from above; HUGE glaciers. And I could see into the ash pit from a completely different vantage point than the day before—it was much better the day before, up close. I could see Mt. Meru off in the distance. It was a beautiful, clear morning. We have been incredibly fortunate with weather. It's been cold, of course, but that's to be expected at this elevation. So it was quite beautiful and I took a lot of video.*

Then we started to make our way down and boy was that fun! The trail that most people take up is a steep, long, 100% scree hill and what we ended up doing was, well, we skied down. We had our poles and our feet and thank goodness for gaiters! When Wilson saw that I was enjoying it and I told him I was, he looked for places where we could do more, faster. When we'd come to a big rock in the middle of our trail, then of course we'd have to slow down and step around it but "dust be damned." It was exhilarating to ski down on my feet from the summit of Mt. Kilimanjaro on scree.

Here's my theory: the reason that Uruhu peak might be smaller is because there is all of this scree on the side and trekkers are pushing it down as we all walk up or scree down.

I saw a lanky young man, well over six feet tall and perhaps late teens or early twenties—didn't look old enough to shave yet— being escorted by two porters, one on each arm to steady him as he struggled with his swaying gait. If I didn't know any better I'd think the poor guy was drunk, but it was altitude sickness and this kid was in bad shape. We watched him approach, asked if we could offer any assistance, but the porters told us they would bring him down.

So that was the beginning of the descent. We met our crew for lunch at Barafu Camp and I'm glad we didn't stay there. It was exposed and crowded, clearly a popular camp and probably quite busy. Seeing this, I was again grateful for the isolation and peace of our route. Then we had a nice two hour walk back through some pretty alpine desert and into the moorland at the very end, and now we're checked in at Millennium Camp. I'm looking around at all of these bushes and flowers, moss and the clouds are coming up out of the rain forest. It's absolutely beautiful. It's been quite an adventure.

Getting closer to Millennium Camp we passed a weathered but serviceable "Kilimanjaro Express taxi" along the side of the trail; it's basically a gurney with four handles and two or four sturdy but well-worn tires. Get AMS and you get to ride down in the Kilimanjaro Express taxi. We also passed a well-maintained helicopter pad just above the camp, also used for rescues. I was vaguely reminded of the travel insurance I purchased before leaving home. I confirmed with myself once again that it was well worth the few hundred dollars for the peace of mind. It would have paid for helicopter evacuation if I'd needed it. I remain incredibly thankful I did not.

Along the way Honest shared with me the news from SENE headquarters. He'd been in contact with them each day, providing updates on our progress. I'd seen him most afternoons standing away from the group, on a high point where he was able to get a signal and I'd watch, holding my breath, afraid he'd get news that my mother had died. I'd barely acknowledged this to myself until that very moment (lest it actually happen) and all of a sudden the flood gates that had been holding that emotion back opened up and the tears flowed, freely and quietly. I kept walking and thinking about home.

I explained briefly to Honest and Wilson why I was crying, telling them not to worry. We hadn't talked about it at all; they hadn't known about my mother's battle with the brain tumor, about her choice to stop treatment, about all that she'd been through since the diagnosis, about how much I want her to be proud of me, about how desperately sad I was that she was dying. I hadn't talked about it at all.

Before I knew it, we'd arrived at the camp. The whole team greeted me when we arrived. In fact, they saw us before I saw them and it was their celebration song that guided me in. They sang to me in Swahili and the tune of it (if not the words) comes easily to mind even now. Smiling and joining in on the dancing

130

was surreal; I was still wearing the emotional cloak of remembering what was happening at home. Stranger still, I felt like my big celebration had been in the crater and so the memory of this serenade is tinged with the bittersweetness of coming down, of knowing soon that I'd be saying good bye. I wanted to enjoy each and every moment of it while I was still here.

I leaned my pack against a rock outside my tent, and then crawled inside to retrieve my Crocs shower shoes from the duffel bag. By the time I'd found them and crawled back out (about a minute), one of the porters had delivered a tub of warm water and the little bar of soap. I leaned over and washed my face; splashing away the layers of dust from the trail was SO nice. Then I found a wonderful rock to sit on, just outside my tent and facing in to our camp (I am convinced that my team planned these conveniences whenever they determined where to put my tent). I sat down and proceeded to remove my dusty gaiters, boots and socks, then to soak my grungy feet in the warm water. Ahhh!

All "camp clean," I sat down solo at my Kikoi-covered table for tea, with Stedman's book and my notebook for company. I wasn't solo for long, however. Within a few minutes I had a visitor, someone I'd met earlier that day on the trail. I'd seen a group on the trail during both the ascent and descent today; they passed us going up to the summit from the crater. They'd asked me about my UPenn cap, and I'd heard from my guides that this group had actually carried a bottle of champagne to the summit!

Dariya, the only female member of this Russian-American trekking group of four, had come over to my camp to introduce herself and to visit. I learned she'd be attending Temple Dental School in the fall, which is within an hour of my home. I gave her my contact information and invited her to come to the house for dinner when she needed a break from studies. Plus, she's about Chip's age and maybe she knows some nice, outdoorsy girls?

*   *   *

[From my recording] *It is our final night on the mountain, and we are now just above 12,000 feet, descended from over 19,000 feet. It's funny, we're just above the rain forest and the clouds have rolled into camp and it's misty, but I can again see that carpet of stars in the sky above. And usually on my 2 or 3 or 4 a.m. bathroom break, when I go out—which I postpone as much as possible because it's been so cold—I get to take a look. Tonight it was actually comfortable with my down jacket and boots. Being comfortable allowed me a chance to stand out there and stare up a while longer.*

Tonight there is a fine mist in the air and the small windows on my tent are covered with a thin layer of condensation. It reminds me of what the tent looked like two nights ago when there was frost on the outside of it.

The clouds are coming in around camp, generated by the rainforest giving up its moisture. I wonder if someone else, some other Kili adventurer, is looking down on this layer of clouds as I had done just a few nights ago.

I had frost on the outside of my tent when we stayed at about 15K feet. When I woke up in the morning at Arrow Glacier Camp, I had frost on both the inside and the outside of my tent. Now what's interesting is that I've got a double layer tent, and despite that, all my water froze. There is an inner tent for me, and then an outside fly layer that actually extends beyond the personal sleeping space, to create a covered landing where you can put your shoes. It's a small landing area that can be zipped up from the inside, or outside. I wonder if it's designed this way to create an air cushion around the tent itself, in addition to creating a barrier for rain, sleet and snow. So yes, on that very cold night, there was actually frost on the inside of the personal space as well as on the outside of the tent.

Tonight we had a delicious lamb stew with fresh carrots, ginger and garlic, and brown rice and green beans that someone

132

brought up from town—the office restocked us with fresh veggies and food and meat. Now I'm full and it's time to settle in for the night.

What I remember most about that double frost on the tent that night is that I was weirded-out because we were at Arrow Glacier Camp, and we were about to do the western breach and I was nervous about it. I froze my butt off that night. You'd think the nervousness would have warmed me up!

DAY 12

[From my SENE itinerary] *Millennium Camp (12,530') to Mweka Gate (5,380'), 8.5 miles; Mbahe Village Farm Cottages. "Our last day is another descent of 7,000 feet with 4 to 5 hours of hiking to the trailhead at Mweka Gate. The trail is steep in places and within the forest may be slippery if wet. At the gate we will temporarily say goodbye to our mountain crew and enjoy a hearty picnic lunch. The trip leaders will take you back to SENE's Mbahe Village Farm for a hot shower and a celebration dinner with the whole team."*

On this, the last day on the trail, I was eagerly looking forward to a shower. At the same time, I was sad to be leaving the trail, to be leaving this mountain. We woke up early and I sat in the cold mountain morning one last time, seated at my special table and looking up at the most-photographed side of the peak, as the light of day grew. I can't remember now what I had for breakfast, though the picture of it reminds me it was probably fresh fruits, eggs, thick slices of whole grain toast with peanut butter & jelly, and tea with warm milk and Killerbee honey.

What I remember most clearly is the feeling of that last morning. It was a camp, with lots of other tents spread around, but there was a sense of privacy from an abundance of bushes in between each of them. The usual hustle and bustle of the morning breakdown felt different on that morning in my memory of it. It was still and quiet. I wondered if perhaps I wasn't the only one relishing the last morning on the mountain.

According to my recording, it was misty.

*   *   *

[From my recording] *Today's descent: up early, finally warm in my sleeping bag and didn't want to get out of it but I had to, and so I did. Since we were at the base of Kilimanjaro, my breakfast table was outdoors, as it was now warm enough. My seat was situated to be staring up at the side of the mountain that is most often photographed. I have to say it again: I am so very pleased to have taken this route; it has been ideal.*

We started on our way today, travelling through the rain forest, which was much more humid and misty than it had been on the way in, via the Lemosho Crater route. In fact, when I woke up, the whole ground was covered in mist from the rain forest.

Traversing from moorland to rainforest was so nice to do in the mist, and it started to rain lightly near the end, apropos since we were in a rainforest. I saw giant ferns; one frond alone was taller than me. I saw a brilliant green patch of clover and thought of my sister-in-law Stacey, who loves Ireland; I passed on taking a picture since we were moving well at that point.

There was a huge group of people on the trail; we heard them before we saw them. 28 trekkers, mostly students from Ireland, some of their teachers, a couple of doctors who were parents, and 120 porters!

I stopped twice to speak with members of the group along the trail. First I spoke with a teenaged boy, who told me they'd raised money as part of this trip; they'd raised a lot actually, to buy equipment for the local hospital. The purchase was inspired by a friend of theirs from school who'd died because the local hospital didn't have the equipment to save her. They were also raising money for a teacher who had M.S. According to this student, a man had spoken to 14 different schools across Ireland, telling them about mountain climbing and how much fun it is.

Next on the trail I met that man. Ian McShe??? I lost his card on the way out, but he wants to meet Simon and so I want to remember to make that introduction because it could be beneficial for everyone involved. When I met Ian, he told me that he's training to break a Kili running record—not the full ascent/descent, just the descent part, and wants Simon to call him (Simon Mtuy, SENE owner, is the original record holder on Kilimanjaro), so I've got to get that information to Simon.

What else about today? When we came out of the rainforest it was muddy, it was muddy most of the way down, and on the way out it was 45 minutes of this road with muck several inches deep—the kind your boots sink into and then they make a sucking noise when you lift them out. SO glad I wasn't doing the whole climb in rain!

When we reached the gate it was crowded, and not with hikers or crew but with a lot of people just hanging around, some selling trinkets. The scene felt dangerous, and I was advised by the crew to stay close to them. They shepherded me through the crowds and even stood guard while I had lunch at a lone little Kikoi-covered table, set up on a staircase just outside one of the buildings. It was elevated, with a view overlooking the busy-ness. I remember savoring sundried tomatoes in oil—definitely new from the farm—bread, and soup, of course, and asking one of the porters from my team to please eat the chicken so it wouldn't go to waste.

Then I went with Honest to the office to get my official certificate, which he held to present to me later. Everything turned out to be just fine.

The whole crew piled into a big, white van, equipment and all, and off we went on the drive back to Mbahe Farm. We stopped in at the office so I could retrieve my "bra liners" of cash, passport, and other papers they'd kept for me. We exchanged the van for Land Rovers. Some of the men stayed behind and others came along in the Land Rover with me. We took much of the equipment with us, which surprised me, and continued on our way out to Simon's farm.

We passed now familiar sites: Moshi, office buildings, the roundabouts, and as we got nearer to the farm we drove through smaller towns, past coffee plantations, and schools. We dropped off Honest at his home, and the others came the rest of the way out to the farm, where they'd stay. They would stay for the party and overnight. I learned that the next day they would clean, dry and inventory all of the equipment.

The energy in the car was fading, as everyone was tired and, for the men, they were closer to home and to their families. I was just tired, dusty, and for the first time, my feet hurt. Eventually we pulled up to the memorial bridge where the road ended, about half a mile down a hill from Mbahe Farm. We stopped, piled out, and were greeted by several bright-eyed boys and girls, here to help carry. Some of the men were pointing to the kids and it was instantly apparent to me that these were their children, come to welcome Dads home. It was sweet; a nice reunion. I followed Wilson up the rocky, uneven trail to the farm and stepped gingerly; my feet did hurt.

Through the gate and back "home" on the farm I dropped my backpack and walking sticks on the porch, and asked the porters to leave the duffel just inside the door. I sat down on the porch step to take off my mud- and muck-covered boots, since I didn't dare track all this mud into the clean cottage.

Next stop: the shower!

That shower was fabulous. Never mind that it took the water some time to warm up. I piled my dusty trail clothes on the floor and cherished the cool feel of the tile on my tired feet while I waited for the water to warm up. Never mind that the water pressure was low, or that there was no easy place to set the hand-held shower head; I found a way to loop it over something on the wall and it worked, intermittently, for almost all of the shower. There was a small, round bar of soap from Zanzibar, black with sloughing pieces in it and well-suited for a gritty body. That soap smelled like cloves and licorice; it was delicious and made juggling the shower head absolutely worth every drop.

I allowed myself the simple gift of appreciation for the warm water flowing over me. For this shower, I didn't turn the water off to soap up before rinsing. I didn't try to be efficient about it as I'd been before. I enjoyed the view of the cottages below from my little shower window, small, with elaborate metal work, that window was the only source of light into the bathroom. I'd learned when I arrived that the farm was literally at the very end of the electric line, and so the bare and barely illuminating overhead bulb received just a dribble of power.

* * *

[From my recording] *Out of the shower and clean! I looked in the mirror, and realized that my nose is terribly sunburned and it hurts. My hands are sunburned and they hurt. Actually both are badly sunburned; I have blisters on my nose and hands. And a strange rash has broken out where my boots hit above the ankles, so I applied cortisone cream and hope it'll kick in.*

Sunburn and blisters were the extent of my injuries, which I consider to be quite fortunate. I had big blisters on the outside of each big toe, compliments of the rainforest "steps" made into the trail on our way out. No wonder my feet hurt. The steps on the trail are, as Stedman said, wonderful in preventing erosion on the trails—clearly an issue in many places—but they were tough on the knees and obviously my big toes didn't like them much. Slick and slippery when wet, as they were for our descent, my hiking poles came in handy and I remembered what Stedman advised, "Use the hiking poles; your knees will thank you." All this stepping down made for quite a different rub in my boots and the last 45 minutes of that muddy road were tiresome and with sore feet. I complained to Honest while we were on the muddy trail, who asked if we should amputate.

In my new role as independent and resourceful Jane Goodall of the Jungle, I sterilized my sewing needle, using a match and antibacterial hand sanitizer, then lanced each big blister. A dab of antibiotic cream and a second skin bandage, et voila! I am back in business. It was time to get ready for the party.

I chose the perfect party dress: the one I bought in Burundi. I slipped on the matching necklace, remembering the sales woman and Jeanne and Burundi, and wrapped myself in a colorful pareo, hand-painted with turquoise, yellow, and pink tropical fish against a black background. I love this pareo; Alan bought it for me on our honeymoon. It didn't match, but it didn't matter, since the colors were lively and the fabric felt cool and soft on my skin. I slipped on my "dress shoes" to complete the outfit.

I felt strangely naked wearing a long skirt instead of pants, and to walk around in open-toed wedge sandals, after wearing double wool socks and hiking boots for so many days.

Feeling clean, light and airy, I grabbed my phone from the charger and made my way out to the dining area, selecting my favorite big chair next to the fireplace. Calculating the time, I called Alan at the office and got voicemail. I called him on cell, got voicemail. I called back to the office and zeroed out to speak to Kristin and deliver the news: "I made it!! Please tell Alan for me so he'll know, and especially since I'm not sure what the phone will want to do on the next part of this journey."

Then I called my sister in Florida and told her, "I made it!!" She told me that Mom was holding steady and I asked her to get the word to Mom and the rest of the family that I had not fallen off the mountain or been eaten by a wild animal or any other crazy thing. She said I sounded out of it, thrilled, exhausted and elated, all at the same time. The call dropped abruptly; the SIM card had run out of time. I hoped my sister would realize what had happened and wouldn't worry.

The blisters on my feet healed up after about a week. The blisters on my nose dissipated after I peeled about three times which was painful to experience and probably disgusting to look at. Thank goodness my little mirror cracked and I didn't have to look at myself too much. Sorry to everyone else.

The strangest injury—and this was as bad as it got for me—was to my thumbs; to the nail beds, to be exact. My thumb nails were sore to the touch for a couple of weeks, but they looked fine; I couldn't see any discoloration, only dirt. For starters, it took about two weeks to completely clean all of the dirt out from under my fingernails, which I'd manicured down to minus. Once home, the texture of the skin under my thumbnails changed and the nail began to lift and separate from the nail bed.

I used the Internet to research the condition when I got home, something I'd become more practiced with after Mom was diagnosed. When she was first diagnosed, I got a huge amount of information from the Internet about her tumor, and about the drugs she was taking. During one overnight in the hospital, I sat with her as she slept. Her brainwaves were being monitored by a machine that displayed them on a small screen. There was concern that she'd had mini-strokes, and as I watched the eight plus lines jump up and down, I feared the worst. The nurses assured me that she was not having mini-strokes, but I wanted to understand what I was seeing on that monitor because it sure looked like erratic activity to me. It's amazing what you can find online.

So I did the same for myself and researched my symptoms. Was it some tropical bacteria that had leeched under the nail in the dirt? I was walking around organic farms and piles of nature's fertilizer, after all. In Burundi, there was discussion of a nasty water-born snail that can get under the skin; it lives in still bodies of water. I hadn't spent any time in the pool or the lake, but maybe I'd been exposed to it another way?

Research calmed my monkey-mind. Again.

Thanks to online pictures and research, my diagnosis was trauma to the nail bed from sunburn. The anti-malarial pills I'd taken for travel in Burundi and the Serengeti make a person highly sensitive to the sun, and I had to take them for 60 days, while walking on a mountain in thin cloud cover, near the equator. Except for the time I spent climbing the western breach and the summit—when I wore gloves—my hands were exposed, including a lot of time with hiking poles, where my thumb was positioned on top, smiling straight up at the equatorial-strong sun.

Why only the thumbnails? Yes, it is strange. I was fascinated by the grow-out pattern on both thumbnails for months. Eventually they did grow out vs. fall off. The last bit of abnormal curvature went the way of the nail clipper a full eight months after my return.

*   *   *

Before I left home I told Mom about Linda Till's comment, that she would have packed extra winter coats to give to the men. Having seen what they wore on the trail, I understood better and agreed. My team seemed well equipped and well covered, but I could see that porters from other teams were not so warmly or well covered. China (pronounced chee-nah), one of the porters on my team, spent several evenings wrapped in a red Masaai shawl and I thought he must have been cold.

Years ago I traded coats with my sister, Jennifer. She got a tan suede jacket from me, and I was the recipient of a super-warm, men's down jacket in bright blue, from her. Very big and fluffy looking, the coat had been Mom's, and she used to call it the big blue marble coat because that's what the wearer resembled, a big blue marble. I loved it—a winter go-to coat for shoveling, getting the mail, playing with the dog. It was a work horse. With Mom's permission, I brought the big blue marble to Kilimanjaro to give away.

I told Alan the story of Linda Till's wish, too, and he gave me the okay to bring a nice but older down ski jacket that he no longer wore or needed. On their own, these coats would have taken up an entire suitcase, but with the air expelled from them thanks to the large and incredibly effective plastic zip bags, they fit into the bodybag-sized travel duffel easily. Same for the sleeping bag. And all of my clothes. So efficient! How about a virtual high-five on that?

After the refreshing shower and burning up the last of my cell phone minutes, I had another important task. The very next thing was to find Alexander, who carried the bio-commode for me the whole way, to offer him a choice of jackets. Which blue down coat would he like? Then I found China and offered the big blue marble to him. I read in Stedman that porters often sell what they receive as gifts to make money; I don't care, as long as it benefits the men and their families.

I couldn't wait to tell my Mom that China, the man who spent freezing nights wrapped in a Masaai shawl, was the beneficiary of the big blue marble.

*　　　*　　　*

[From my recording] *Tonight I am sleeping in a big bed back on Mbahe Farm. It was a nice evening, and a satisfying celebration. Francis Moshi, SENE's General Manager, attended the party in a suit and tie. The whole crew was here minus Katunzi who I hope is okay; he's our chef and I haven't seen him for a couple of days, not since he left with the group that split off before Arrow Glacier Camp.*

The evening included singing and dancing around the table, and speeches. I thanked the team for spending more than a week with me, for working so hard for my adventure-of-a-lifetime. I wished them the joy of reunion with their wives and the gift of more children. Wilson translated for me.

It was a nice night by the fire with a Kilimanjaro beer and hearty traditional food—green bananas cooked with pork which was delicious, and samosas that had a spicy kick. I worked with Francis to understand how the tips would be divvied up.

It's Kili time!

Tipping is crucial on a trip like this. These men had each worked very hard for my benefit and comfort, ensuring my safety and helping to ensure my success. Carry up, set up, cook and clean up, break down and repeat—hey, I do similar work at home every day and have a BIG appreciation for being cared for in this way. They carried water, heated water, and cleaned the utensils in chlorinated water. They sang to me, encouraged me, and shared smiles through sweat along the trail. They spent nine+ days away from their families.

Understanding the protocol and how far my total tip allowance would go was important to me. From what I read, the amount varies. As I understood it, ten percent per person was about average. But I was one person and SENE sent me with a whole crew. I had already planned a 25% tip and had the cash ready to deliver. Only one problem: I didn't have enough small denomination bills to divide up the tips and give them out individually, so the men would have to wait until Francis could break it down in the office the next day.

Francis and I sat in two big chairs by the fire so I could look at the tip sheet and understand who would receive what amount. We listed the names of each of the men on the sheet. Though all of this was done away from the men, I was confident that both Honest and Wilson could hear and understand what was going on.

It was a sliding scale, with the senior guide, second guide and head cook getting the higher amounts and then on down. It included the house staff at Mbahe Farm, which I hadn't taken into account—I was glad they had. According to Francis, it was more than double what they usually get which absolutely pleased me. He said porters would be okay with $40 and these guys were getting $75, so that's not quite double but it's more than usual, and that makes me happy.

The men cheered when he told them and that warmed my heart.

DAY 13

The next morning I enjoyed a hearty farewell breakfast, soaking up the sunshine and delighting in the stunning Variable Sunbirds as they flitted from red flower to red flower. I savored the flavors of the killer Killerbee honey, fresh fruits, omelet and toast. All for me, just for me.

It was a glorious morning and I prepared to leave Mbahe Farm with a sense of complete satisfaction, tinged with a hint of wistfulness. I'd done it; I'd made it to the top of Mt. Kilimanjaro, and via the scariest route. With that sense of achievement, I felt strong, I felt confident. And now it was time to go.

Part of me wished I could be back on the mountain trail again. Part of me missed my family and, having met my big goal, that part of me was ready to be with them again. I wanted to share stories, photos and videos from the adventure with them. A big part of me was ready to go home.

But I would not be going home today—the plan was to see the Great Migration on the Serengeti plains—and so I let the thought of going home simply flutter away like a Variable Sunbird.

Dressed and fully packed, devices charged, and still-damp, hand-washed socks and underwear tucked into a bag at the last minute, it was once again time to go. I met Suah (name changed), my Serengeti safari guide, and then I was off for one final walk through the cow pasture, along the path that took me past a few members of my team. Some of the men had stayed overnight and were now cleaning, drying and checking the supplies from the climb. I waved at the men, higher up on the hill, and wondered as I walked on, if perhaps they were preparing the equipment for the next visitors, and would they be here soon?

I walked along the trail and enjoyed the early morning sun on the trees, the sound of the babbling stream below to my left, and the delightful chatter of school children in their little blue uniforms with white shirts, walking above me to the right on their way to school. I saw Wilson walking home, making his way up and over the hill. I gave him a silent wish for a long and healthy life, and a prolonged wave of thanks and good bye. It was like a scene at the end of a movie.

The Land Rover was waiting for us at the memorial bridge down below. We loaded up the bags—both my duffel and the hard-sided suitcase came along this time—and then I lifted myself into the left-side, front passenger seat. My backpack between my knees, I settled into the seat in preparation for the long ride to the plains.

My guide had a cell phone and it was lively. I soon discovered why: we stopped for a moment in town to pick up a friend of his. After we stopped, he asked if I would mind if we gave his friend a lift. I did mind but what could I say at this point since the guy I didn't know was already in the Land Rover and sitting behind me. They conversed in Swahili as I sat, open-minded but alert. It turned out to be no problem and no big deal; hakuna matata—we dropped the friend off in the next town.

While my guide spent more time on the phone, always in Swahili, I learned that SENE's Owner, Simon Mtuy, wanted to meet me before we travelled out to the Serengeti, and he to Europe to train a marathoner he was working with. I had seen Simon briefly on the road, before the climb, when our cars passed in opposite directions. He was headed to Mbahe Farm with his two little boys and I was enroute to Simba Farm with Josefu and Honest.

Suah's phone calls were to coordinate where we'd meet up with Simon. Soon we pulled into a gated community/hotel just outside town.

The night before, I'd been relieved to find Ian McKeever's business card in a pants pocket; I thought I'd lost it. He wanted to meet Simon, and I'd been hoping for an opportunity to deliver it. I rummaged through my pack to find it and to have it at the ready.

I was pleasantly surprised to see Josefu, who had originally picked me up at the airport and shepherded me through the first couple of days and up to the trailhead. This gave me a chance to say goodbye. I wish I'd been prepared with a tip for him but I wasn't, and so I gave and received a big hug of thanks and appreciation, being sure to tell Simon how much I'd appreciated all that Josefu had done for me.

I sat with Simon in the lobby of the gated building, which was equidistant from the SENE offices and our way out. I gave him Ian's card and relayed the story of the big group of Irish trekkers as well as Ian's wish to speak with him about training for a record-holding descent of the mountain. I shared my deep appreciation for the level of professionalism I'd experienced from his whole team, especially Tim, my guides Honest and Wilson, the house staff, and Josefu. I complimented the food, the village and his farm, and shared with him my appreciation for this wonderful experience.

Simon told me about the wide diversity of work he does to make the experiences of other travelers to Tanzania even better, including affordable, culturally-rich places to stay before and after the climb. He is a dedicated Ambassador for Tanzania and takes that role quite seriously, developing the strength of the national community—its people, its economy—as well as delivering the message beyond its borders of what Tanzania has to offer. Simon is a connector, committed to helping others experience this country he loves and calls home.

I was thrilled to receive two pounds of coffee beans from Simon, direct from his farm. Kilimanjaro coffee, organic from Mbahe Farm, is sweet and mild; Alan said, "It tastes like the milk is already in it." For almost a year now I've been enjoying a private blend: part organic Mbahe Farm beans, part Columbian and part cardamom pods. For coffee purists this may sound sacrilegious but I've had a preference for the pods in my coffee since visiting the Arab Quarter in Jerusalem and I love it. In fact, I think I'll go make another cup right now.

THE SERENGETI

This is a story about Kilimanjaro, but many people, like me, add on a trip to the Serengeti and/or Zanzibar. I'm more a mountain girl than beach-goer so the Serengeti was my choice. Plus, when I saw how close Kilimanjaro was to it—you may remember I had instant recall of James Earl Jones' voice describing the scenery in National Geographic's *The Great Migration*—I knew I had to make the attempt to see it. The timing of my trip made it dicey— would the migration be on the Tanzania side, or would it have moved to Kenya and out of easy reach? This became an important part of my planning—if I was going to go all the way to East Africa, and then to the Serengeti, I wanted to make sure I'd be able to see the Great Migration.

I was also drawn to Ngorongoro Crater and Oldupai Gorge, considered the birthplace of humankind since the discovery of the earliest known human fossils there. I learned that researchers had discovered the oldest female remains in Oldupai, even older than the previously found oldest remains of "man." Actually being there confirmed what I'd originally thought, that this is one of the most important prehistoric sites in the world in advancing the understanding of human evolution.

I made my objectives for this part of the trip just as clear as I did for the Kili climb, and was rewarded with an itinerary that would help me see all that I'd hoped for, and more.

[From my SENE itinerary] *"The Serengeti is probably the most famous wildlife area in the world. Its pure numbers are staggering: about 4 million animals reside within its ecosystem, including a million and a half wildebeest, a quarter million zebras, twice that many gazelle, and tens of thousands of the their predators (lion, leopard, cheetah, hyena, jackal, crocodile, etc.). The Serengeti is also the site of one of the most magnificent events of the natural world—the migration of more than a million wildebeest in a cyclical process that occurs in different stages and areas throughout the year."*

*   *   *

My guide and I made a few stops on the way out for provisions, discussing what we needed to do in advance, and how to be efficient about it since our drive would be a long one. Suah would pick up "lunch boxes," which, he told me, contained fried foods like chicken and donuts.

Oh no . . . this was so utterly unappetizing to me after being pampered with lovingly-prepared organic foods on the farm and on the mountain. I just couldn't do donuts, or fried. "You know what I'd really like?" I told him, "For me, can you just grab some bananas, avocados and salt?"

He liked the idea and agreed. I shared my other basic "need to have" items, beginning with a SIM card for the phone, one that would work on the Serengeti. Then I asked if there was time to stop in a particular shop, *The Blue Heron* in Arusha. The shop had been recommended by the four teachers as the place where I'd probably be able to find the licorice-clove soap I loved so much, and some gifts to bring home. I showed Suah the hand-drawn map of its location and he knew the place well—lots of ex-pats and visitors stay in the hotel there, he told me.

Suah dropped me off at *The Blue Heron*, and we agreed on the time he'd come back for me. I negotiated here—he offered 45 minutes and I asked for 75—the traffic was jammed, after all, and he agreed to the extra time.

The grounds were lively, busy and clearly a nice place to be, with a full outdoor restaurant in front. The shop was high-end and featured regionally-made toys for kids, music, jewelry, kitchenware, linens, and clothing. I wandered around quickly, looking for the soap, but when I asked the clerk I found out that they did not carry soap. C'est la vie; there wasn't a shortage of nice gifts to take home.

I'm not one of those people who feel obligated to buy gifts to bring home for everyone. With my family tree, I'd need more suitcases if I did that every time I travelled. This trip was different though. I wanted those back home to know that I'd thought of them while was away. They may never know just how much, but the fact is that my mother and that branch of the family tree were all very much with me on this trip.

I lingered over the linens—so many fine choices—and had a devil of a time trying to select from the huge, gorgeous plaid piles of Kenyan Kikoi. I could not resist quilted comforters and pillowcase covers in floral pink and maroon patches with tiny little bells all around the edges and similar hair bands from Zanzibar. I looked at the clothing, for something to bring home to my sister, but nothing was quite right. I lusted after the rich wooden food service pieces, but realized they'd never survive the journey home, and so I resisted buying them.

They had a huge selection of handmade toys for children, but what caught my eye was the selection of children's books. Books, I reasoned, would be easy to carry in my luggage and had a good chance of surviving the rest of my journey. Clever children's books with African stories, richly illustrated with animals and children, lined several shelves. As I paged through them, I thought they'd be ideal for my nephews. I wanted my nephews to be exposed to stories they would enjoy, about animals and bravery and kindness. I wanted them to see the children in these stories, who have darker skin and live a different life in another part of the world, yet who play and draw and sing and do kid-things, just like they do. Selecting which books to bring for each of them took as much time as selecting Kikoi.

Though it didn't seem like a place where you'd negotiate a discount, I thought I'd at least ask, since I was spending a few hundred dollars on all of these gifts to bring home. To my delight, they did give me a discount when I asked. Everything fit, neatly and tightly packed, into three grocery-store-type plastic bags, and I didn't even need a ziplock! They would fit into the luggage where the down coats had been.

I finished shopping early; it wasn't yet time for Suah to be back, so I sat at a table in the open-air waiting area between the shop and the restaurant. I had a healthy juice drink, enjoyed the perfect weather, and people watched. I saw families, business people, small groups of girlfriends and one woman who looked like Anne Heche (the movie star who plays the character, Jessica, on the HBO series "Hung"). I wondered about their lives and what it might be like to live and work in Arusha.

The restaurant was bustling with the activity of an international crowd and so was the town: the U.N.'s International Criminal Tribunal, located in Arusha, was in session and had just handed down a ruling that shocked me when I'd read about it. I was in disbelief at the reality of it, disturbed and disappointed. The War Crimes Tribunal had just established the guilt of a mother and her son who'd ordered women raped as part of their war strategy, as part of the genocide in Rwanda. I don't understand how one person can be so cruel to another. Even more incomprehensible to me was the fact that a woman would be the root of such violence against other women.

It reminded me of a Villanova University classroom debate almost a decade ago on the topic of genocide in Rwanda. I was to argue FOR it; I argued against Felicia Rivers, a colleague from work and in class. We stood at podiums in front of the room and began. After a few minutes the Professor interrupted us to ask me, "Which side are you arguing for, anyway?" I was trying, but look; you just can't argue FOR something like genocide, there is no reason for hate.

I saw the green Land Rover pull up, gathered my packages and walked over. It had been a very productive outing for us both: Suah procured a new phone card for me, a case of bottled water (that we will barely make a dent in), and produce from one of the local stands. He told me that the stands closer to where the ex-pats live are more expensive, that he knew where to find the best stands, where the locals go, and he did. What a score too— ostrich egg-sized avocados in varying stages of ripeness, strategically selected to last over a few days; a fat cluster of small *yellow* bananas, an important distinction, since a lot of cooked dishes here feature underripe bananas, which are good for cooking but not so delicious for snacking; and a bag of oranges, too.

We drove out of town and stopped on the roadside, where we found a picnic spot on the ground next to shade-dappled rows of coffee bean plants, to enjoy a delicious lunch. Suah produced a one pound bag of sea salt, the smallest he could find, and used an impressive super-sized Swiss Army knife to open the package. I grabbed the small roll of duct tape from my backpack to seal up the salt bag, so we could continue to use it. I'd also brought along a compact nylon shopping bag, something I'd received at a Wharton Women in Business conference years ago and saved, one of those fabric bags that folds down into a tiny little 2"x2" square, and folds out to carry all kinds of things. It was optimal for our heavy-weight, multi-day lunch box.

He cut the avocado and handed me half. I sprinkled some salt and took a big bite—ahhh! Eating it right out of its own wrapper in big, smushy bites was decadent and delicious. Next, the orange; oranges are nature's best for aromatherapy, delivering a senses-full dose of sunshine, and these did not disappoint. They smelled as good as they tasted. I enjoyed one of the bananas for dessert and then it was time to pack it up and hit the road for the first of many long drives.

That's not a bowling ball, it's an avocado!

We passed from small town to countryside, and eventually into dry plains. The plains here are Masaai land, where little boys no more than my nephew's age of seven or nine were tending huge herds of cattle, and bathing naked in small water retention ponds, right next to the road. In the towns, I saw women in bright, beautiful dresses made from

African fabric, and was inspired to ask Suah if he knew of a good place to stop, to buy some African fabric along the way.

As the light of day was fading, we pulled into a lone but large outdoor-indoor shop with nothing but fabric. Kikoi, Kanga, beautiful batik, all hung for the shopper to see. I used the light from my phone to get a look at the patterns and colors inside the dark shop. They were ready to close, it was getting late and we still had more driving to do, so I worked quickly to select more gifts to bring home. Speed shopping isn't my preference; I find it difficult to decide when faced with so many excellent choices and very little time. Making snap decisions on gifts is like rushing a good meal—you miss the pleasure of savoring each bite.

Nonetheless, I rose to the challenge, finding grape-festooned Kanga for girlfriends, and gorgeous batiks for my sister Karen and her friend, Christine, who is like our sister; they live in Florida and I imagined these would make lovely wraps, befitting the beach. I found two other patterns that were must-have, to make into table linens. I could have spent hours in this place but it was time to move on; it was getting dark and we hadn't reached our destination yet.

The prices were much higher than what I expected, based on what Edit, one of the teachers from Mbahe Farm, had told me. I also knew that negotiation was probably assumed as a way of doing business in this kind of shop. I was in a hurry and so my efforts at negotiation were half-hearted. Besides, I reasoned with myself, this was clearly a family-owned shop, and so I overpaid and didn't give it a second thought.

It was quite dark by the time we pulled off the road and into the lodge, which was sprawling and luxurious. The first stop was the front desk for check-in, and then with the help of a man with a flashlight, I wheeled and lugged my bags to the room, since, as Suah told me, it wasn't smart to leave anything of value unattended in the Land Rover. The room was huge in size and in furnishings, modern and old all at once, with a big fireplace and sliding glass doors looking over a short deck and into the local woods. It wasn't too unlike the view from a ground floor condo at home. The bathroom too was huge, with an open, beautifully tiled shower that was as big as a queen size bed. I showered up after the dusty day's ride, and then it was time for dinner. I retraced my steps on the path to the dining hall, hoping to get there before it closed.

I brought the phone along with me but had no success dialing out; all of the instructions were in Swahili. The next day I'd have to ask Suah for help using it.

On the next night, and the one after, we stayed at Kati Kati Camp, on the Serengeti. Made up of large, well-equipped seasonal tents, it was clearly selected for its location: within striking distance of the Great Migration.

The tents were huge, constructed of sturdy canvass with zip down windows. Each had a covered "front porch" with a side table and two chairs. On the porch, there was a stand with a canvass washbowl in one corner; there was a water pitcher and soap on the table, and an ashtray I would not need. I found a canvass-framed mirror that was sewn into the porch roof; it dropped down at just the right height for someone tall, and when I found it, I imagined Ernest Hemingway using it to shave in the morning.

I took my boots off outside, but Suah advised that I should not leave them, or anything else, outside the tent. I imagined animals coming by to take them at night, or insects crawling into them. I thought of my dog at home who likes to find "objects of mutual interest" like socks or shoes, and then trot away with her prize.

Suah helped me figure out the phone and I was finally able to reach Alan at home on the second Serengeti night. I talked with him from the "front porch" of my safari tent in Kati Kati Camp. It was good to hear his voice, though he sounded tired. He said it was good to hear mine. He said he'd been worried and was glad to hear that I was okay.

After the call I sat outside my tent, watching a wildebeest herd cross in the distance. I enjoyed the peace and quiet as the sun set on the Serengeti Plain. A waiter came by; I asked for a Kilimanjaro beer and put in my request for a shower. The showers in camp are sourced from a tower out back, that collects rainwater. The water is heated on a stove and then delivered to each tent individually by a man who pours a big bucketful into the shower reservoir before he tells the person-in-residence that it's ready.

Although I didn't have it on the mountain, I did now have a small bottle of shampoo. The smell of that shampoo reminded me of home. Alan and I brought it back from a trip to New Zealand, where we'd hiked to Ben Lomond Summit and shared a chocolate bar at the top, while summertime snowflakes fell, to celebrate our ten-year wedding anniversary. The shower was warm, and after washing off the dust of the day, I felt less homesick and more like my contented self again.

Dining with my safari guide on the first night at Kati Kati Camp, the conversation turned to "stepping out," the local phrase for having an affair. It was a harmless conversation yet I woke up the next day with a gut feeling that it wasn't quite appropriate conversation. Having learned the lesson from the red ants on Kilimanjaro, I decided to honor my gut and made an easy adjustment.

When making decisions about what to pack for this trip, I showed my sister, Karen, a favorite shirt to get her opinion; "Should I bring this one, or not?" A man's short-sleeved, size XL, the cream colored shirt featured lots of army green and tan fish in a pattern. It was manly, big and boxy, and I thought it would be perfect for safari. My sister thought that if my intention was to look as unattractive as possible, this was the shirt to wear. After the conversation about stepping out, I wore that shirt every day for the rest of the Safari.

*   *   *

The drives from park to park were long, dusty, and bumpy thanks to miles and miles of washboard dirt roads. Eight hours of jostling and bumps and dust and sun. For most of the way I was hugging my boobs to hold them in place (no bra would ever be enough on a road like this) and trying to keep my severely sunburned hands covered at the same time. They call it an African massage.

This is Masaai land and we passed huge old trucks carrying livestock, and often people who were hanging on and off the sides, back and top. Each time we passed one of these trucks we'd roll up our windows—literally, by hand—so that we didn't choke on all of the dust from the road.

Sometimes we drove on the opposite side of roads because the ride was smoother there. I knew my guide was doing what he could, but this part was intolerable and I got cranky, wishing I'd flown into the park, which had been an option. It would have been a much more pleasant and efficient journey if I'd flown in.

Being in the Serengeti with local residents, both large and small, from carnivores to scorpions, who like to bite, made it a dangerous place to pull over if we needed a pit stop. With that in mind, I avoided drinking too much water if the ride would be long because I didn't want to have to relieve myself next to the door of the Land Rover, along the road, with the guide as lookout. My water consumption on the Serengeti was significantly less than what it was on Mt. Kilimanjaro.

Walking every day on Kilimanjaro was delightful, and always with purpose. I can't tell you what Zanzibar is like, but I can tell you that spending all day, every day in a Land Rover, after being allowed to walk so much, is not easy. On the Serengeti, I couldn't walk anywhere of much distance because it was just too dangerous.

The grounds at the first hotel had long, winding paved walkways, and a guide with a flashlight to escort visitors after dark. The best walk I had was around the small paved driveway of the hotel, on my final morning in Africa. The guard there let me walk a few hundred feet beyond the gate, but I was called back quickly; he told me that a black leopard had been spotted in the area, meaning I wasn't safe going too far beyond his view.

It was in this hotel, on the edge of Ngorongoro Crater, that I was woken up in the middle of the night by the sounds of something just outside my window. I heard contented munching and the splat of elimination. Whatever it was, it was outside my room, on the other side of the low-to-the-ground, open but screened window, and literally six feet from where I lay. It was dark, I had no idea what time it was, and I didn't want to check my watch because as soon as the animal came into my awareness, I obviously came into his or hers, and it stopped munching. I turned my head to look out the window and the animal moved along on its way. Without my glasses I couldn't get a good look (I'm nearsighted); I only knew that whatever it was, it was as big as a cow and very dark. Suah told me the next day that it was probably a cape buffalo, quite harmless and clearly enjoying the cool hillside grasses at night.

I remembered an evening in South Africa, on a trip with Alan, where we'd been instructed never to walk back to our room without a guide, who always carried a gun and a flashlight. Ready early one morning, I stepped outside to walk to breakfast while Alan showered, and was immediately greeted by the roar of a lion, "I am the king of the jungle! Huh, huh, huh, huh." When you hear the roar, you can hear the lion saying this. Seriously. Regaining my intelligence, I quickly turned on my heel and took the three or four steps back into our room and shut the door. I waited until Alan was ready, and then called for an escort to take us both to breakfast. I found out later that the lion I'd heard was over a mile away but the sound of that roar, the feel of it, came through the air and the ground in deep, palpable waves; so strong, it could have been right next to me.

Back on the Serengeti, we were on a game drive and the Land Rover was stopped on the side of the road. I was standing on the backseat with my head popped out of the roof. It was an exceptional stop—I was delighted to be watching lion cubs jumping like kittens in the tall grass. Truly delight-full[19]. In that moment of watching pure, carefree joy, I felt and heard an out of place, low, deep rumble. I looked at my guide and asked quietly, "Was that you?" Sotto voce, he replied, "No, it is the Mama, she is beneath the car."

Sure enough, we were parked over a medium-sized drainage pipe that passed under the road from one part of the plain to the next, and out from it, directly beneath the car, Mama sauntered to corral her cubs. Suah explained to me in a very quiet voice that there were three cubs in this group (I'd only seen two so far) and Mama was headed out to a patch of trees just a short distance away to fetch the straggler. We watched and I videotaped as the small family was brought together again, the cubs leaping in the grass and following Mama back to her spot, in the drain pipe under the car. She waited as the cubs filed in and looked up at me with red-rimmed, bloodshot eyes. I imagined that they were the tired eyes of a Mother who was keeping track of her little balls of energy, even though she may have been up all night, hunting to feed her little ones, and so she didn't sleep. My eyes looked at her in awe.

*   *   *

The sights I saw in the Serengeti were simply amazing and every day I wished that Alan could have been with me. He was travelling for business and so I was on my own for this last part of the adventure, just me and my guide in a Land Rover that I couldn't drive since I don't drive a stick shift.

---

[19] Intentional spelling. These cubs radiated delight, and to me, the entire scene was simply full of their joy; it was inescapably contagious.

[From my notebook] *25 June 2011, near the end of the Serengeti travel: My guide asked me to count, and so we did, to discover that during this trip I have seen 52 lions! Three cheetahs, one leopard cub, cape buffalo, hyenas, hippos and warthogs; the Great Migration of wildebeests and zebras, and more birds than I can count, so magnificent in purples, blues, greens, yellows, red, white and black and gray and brown. I have seen elephants, giraffes, gazelles, jackal, and a Serval cat—spotted, sleek and regal, the type of pet I'd imagine Cleopatra would have chosen.*

All along I've been moved by gratitude for what I've seen in this magical place. I approached each day with no expectations, only openness to whatever might come our way. Counting the sightings seemed greedy to me, and I'm sure my guide knew this on some level; perhaps that's why we only counted at the end.

The word I'd use to describe the Great Migration is: expansive. Mixed up herds of wildebeest and zebras were grazing as far and wide as my eyes could see. Instinctively they follow the grasses and the water in a huge elliptical pattern designed by Mother Nature. What I saw of these grunting, squeaking herds (you can hear them in the videos) was quite different from the intense cattle-chute river crossing scenes they show in the NatGeo program, and that was okay with me. I saw them moving in clumps, seemingly without any real purpose or reason; when one decided to move, a cluster followed, usually with a start and a jerk. My guide told me they're actually not very smart, the Wildebeests, and that it's astonishing they've survived in such prodigious numbers. That said, we saw evidence that they do make quite a smorgasbord for local predators. We saw packs of vultures picking at remains and sun-bleached skulls along the roadside.

*　　*　　*

The Ngorongoro Crater is like a piece of heaven here on earth. I wondered, is this what Eden was like? My guide explained the uniqueness of the place while we were watching zebras, hundreds of them. They were enjoying the afternoon, some happily scratching their bodies on the dirt wall leading up from a stream; it was idyllic. He explained that these zebras were clearly born here, in Ngorongoro Crater; he can tell because they have no fear of standing in the water, like zebras in the open Serengeti do. They were crossing the stream without care. The reason: there are no crocodiles here. He explained that only animals that are able to migrate up and over the wall and down into the crater can live in it. Crocodiles can't make that trek.

[From my SENE itinerary] *"Go for a game drive on the famed Ngorongoro Crater, which is often referred to as "Africa's Eden." The descent into the crater, 2,500 feet below the rim, is an unforgettable experience. Its 100 square miles is home to almost 30,000 animals, creating a density and diversity of wildlife unseen anywhere else in Africa. Ngorongoro is the best location for viewing the rare black rhino and to observe huge old bull elephants who come here to "retire."*

My guide explained another type of migration to me. He told me that this is a place where the old ones come to die. Old bull elephants and grand old cape buffalo. We saw a few of these old gents, including a cape buffalo known to the locals as *The General*.

[From my recording] *This afternoon, at the end of the day in Ngorongoro crater, we waited for a black rhino. For 45 minutes. But he didn't want to get up from his cozy napping spot, so we moved on.*

I've seen a lot of hyenas and I've heard them each night at camp; they've been very close by. They say the hyenas are what I hear going by my tent at night, rubbing against the cloth wall. Coming into camp today we met a hyena napping under a tree immediately next to the road. His belly was round and full, quite obvious as he lay sprawled out on his side. When we approached, he lifted his head up, smiled for the picture (I kid you not— look at his toothy smile in the photo), and then lay back down to rest, content after a good meal.

Later, I watched two jackals work together to get a baby Thompson gazelle. One jackal had the baby by the neck in its little jaw and the mother gazelle chased it. The second jackal worked to distract her. It was a quick death; I watched the little tail wagging furiously as the life left its jugular. I wiped away a few tears and asked my guide to drive on. Seeing one kill was enough, but I know that this is the law of nature, and life on the Serengeti is as hard and violent as it is beautiful and serene. The herbivores graze and the carnivores stalk and pounce; this is the rhythm of life in the Serengeti.

This morning we saw four male lions walking together outside Kati Kati camp, a very rare sight indeed. Even my guide took his camera out for that one. They walked right across our path. Watching them saunter across the road, I imagined they were four guys who'd been out on the town the night before. They were taking their time going home; the four of them walking in a single file line, making their way early in the morning after what I imagined, with a smile, must have been a rowdy night.

In Ngorongoro we saw part of a pride that had probably just finished a meal; they were napping in the sun with full, round bellies. Amazingly, some of the lionesses were lying on their backs, bellies exposed and paws splayed. Cubs nudged and cuddled and played around close to them. On day one of my Safari, I saw a lioness with her two teenagers, a boy and a girl, sleeping in a tree at Lake Manyara. We saw the Mama first—she was much easier to spot—then her two teenagers sleeping on branches below her. Though they all appeared to be sleeping, it was clear from their positioning, and her view, that she was watching over them.

The four males sauntered freely, out in the open. Females sprawled, belly up after their meal, feeling safe and content yet totally exposed in an open area. They were satisfied. As Kings and Queens of the jungle, they feared nothing.

A pride of 12 divides. We watch them and they watch the buffalo. It's a big opportunity and they are waiting patiently. One big score will feed the entire pride. One small mistake (to be downwind or move too soon) may alert the buffalo to their presence and then everybody has to wait and plan for the next opportunity.

Lions: they fear nothing. They have big patience.

*   *   *

If you were an animal, which would you be?

We asked this question during the leadership conference in Burundi. In the moment, I chose the golden retriever for its qualities of being loyal, fun and playful. Before that, however, I liked the salmon image: strong and determined. I used to say I was a salmon, always swimming upstream against the current. On Mt. Kilimanjaro I asked my guide, Wilson, which animal he would be. "I am a lion" he told me, "King of the jungle, strong and fearing nothing."

On the Serengeti, I watched the lionesses with particular interest, watched them hunt, care for their cubs, lounge in community. I listened to the stories told by my safari guide. To expose the belly is a very trusting move; the animal is vulnerable and will only do it when they feel completely safe. He told me, while we watched them work, that the lioness is patient and waits for just the right moment. Expending tremendous energy in a kill, she doesn't want to waste energy unnecessarily, or scatter the target herd. The lioness is strategic, forming alliances within the pride. They work together for the goal of feeding their family. Their family is their pride.

I remember my first safari, watching a lioness move across the plain under a hot midday sun, panting to cool herself in the heat, her pace deliberate. I know that rhythm from lessons I learned about how to approach a horse: how to observe the horse visually and how to walk around them in a confident cowgirl way that has a rhythm like the lioness. It's the same rhythm I felt when I wore my new backpack on Mt. Kilimanjaro with the weight evenly resting on my hips; I felt grounded, firm, and confident. The rhythm is easy and kind of sexy, it's calming, not hurried, and it's a walk with attitude from inner strength that says, "Yeah, I've got this."

GOING HOME

The journey home began with a six-hour long African massage—a dusty, bumpy drive back through and out of the Serengeti, past Masaai lands, herds and boy herders. We saw brightly dressed parishioners walking to and from church. We even saw a parade of a hundred or more worshippers singing a hymn that inspired me to clap along. Though I didn't understand their words, I felt the joy, and their singing was a bright spot in this very long ride from Ngorongoro Crater to Kilimanjaro airport (JRO).

The first flight was from JRO back to Adidas Ababba (ADD) in Ethiopia, where severe, dramatic lightning storms delayed our departure. The terminal, designed like a hangar with its tall, buttressed roof of rounded steel, was familiar to me, since I'd been there just a few weeks earlier. The building had windows high up and all around, providing an excellent observatory for the brilliant flashes of lightning against the pitch-black sky. Travelling through this airport the first time, I'd been chatty and interested in connecting with fellow travelers. But this time was different, I was different. I was leaving the cocoon of Africa; I was withdrawing.

There were elaborately dressed women behind me in line, who had a sense of personal space that was, clearly, different from my sense of it. They were bumping into me and into my backpack, their shoes were hitting into the backs of my boots. It was harmless but annoying. I felt jostled, pushed, and I wished for peace, more personal space and some breathing room, please. I could feel myself starting to close up in "protect" mode, harnessing energy that might otherwise fly out in a not-so-pleasant way.

Weary from the day's travel, I didn't feel I had much patience to spare. I sat in the waiting area with very little interest in conversation. I think I was, on some level, steeling myself, preparing to go back home to responsibility and family strife. The adventure was nearing its end and I was sad to be leaving Africa.

That attitude of keeping to myself stayed with me until almost the end of the flight from ADD to DC, when, for some reason, I started talking with a young man across the aisle from me. We talked about why we'd each been in Africa and discovered that we'd both climbed Kilimanjaro. We talked about what kind of animal we'd be and why. We talked about literature, reading, and writing. He seemed to me an old soul in a young man's body, wise with tangible positive energy. I felt recharged by that conversation. The melancholy of an adventure ending, of saying goodbye to Africa, all of it had resolved, and now I was both ready and looking forward to reengaging with my world.

We landed at Dulles airport, in Washington, DC, mid-morning on a Monday. The brief layover in DC included reading through a long, long list of emails, and the ending of my brief time as a vegetarian. I enjoyed a cheeseburger, fries and a thirst-quenching Bloody Mary, while I read through those emails. The last flight of the journey home took me to Philadelphia International Airport for an early afternoon arrival. I collected my suitcase and duffel, and then hopped into the next-in-line cab for the ride home.

That first step into the house after being away is always a nice experience for me; I like the way home smells. I dropped my bags, took off my hiking boots and the dusty clothes that I'd had on for too many hours to count, and enjoyed a long, hot shower. It was nice to get home in the middle of the day—it was about 3:00 p.m. local time—which meant I could take my time reimmersing. My mail was waiting for me; Alan had put it all together in a bin. But I wasn't ready to go through it yet . . . it would still be there tomorrow. I didn't unpack either.

Alan came home and it was so good to see his smiling face! My puppy came home next and, quite strangely, she didn't acknowledge me. After five minutes she obviously forgave me for being away for so long, and came over to play. My sister Karen arrived from Florida, as scheduled, the next day. Life returned to its normal, faster pace.

Visits to see Mom were coordinated and I brought pictures, videos and gifts. I told stories about the Big Blue Marble and the whole adventure. In sharing stories, I consciously tempered my energy and enthusiasm, making an effort to minimize what might be negative reactions to it. Although no one in the family had an interest to travel to Africa, or to climb, and even though I know it was easier back home with me out of the way for a while, I was, nonetheless, keenly aware that they'd all been here taking care of her. I thought it best to rein in the enthusiasm.

I started to hold back on talking about the trip in other spheres too, when I noticed that other people were willing to hear about it, but only for a few minutes before losing interest. I thought it strange—to me, this was an incredibly exciting adventure—but the conversational cues to end the conversation (changing the subject, attention waning) were obvious and undeniable. I certainly didn't want to be one of those people who could only hold a conversation about one topic. I didn't want people to think, "Oh no, here comes Deb. She'll talk your ear off about Mt. Kilimanjaro." I suppose I'd contributed to this by taking the journey alone.

Dinners were planned with friends and family we hadn't seen in over a month. Karen said I was more exhausted than I realized, hitting the wall early during that first week home. One night I left the dinner table while it was still full of our guests; good friends who, thankfully, understood it was jet lag. I don't remember being especially tired after that first week back, but I do remember the emotional exhaustion.

I stopped exercising and gained another ten pounds. I kept on giving blood, there was no choice if I wanted to see Mom, and the scar tissue mounted. I started a meditation practice.

Mom had made a list of things she wanted to do before she died and she'd completed it months ago. With the list complete, there was nothing left to do but to make peace where she could and to enjoy life's moments.

There was a calm, settled presence around Mom her last few months; I believe she'd found that peace.

My mother died on October 1, 2011, three full months after I returned from Africa and a full 17 months after being diagnosed with a terminal brain tumor. She was with us for much longer than any of us had hoped.

Excerpts from my eulogy for Mom, read at her Memorial Service on October 7, 2011

Mom loved her family—especially her beautiful grandchildren— and her friends.

She kept Karen and me connected to our little sister and brothers with pictures and cards; making sure we always knew we were big sisters.

Karen and I grew up in upstate NY with our father, and visited our Mom in the summer; then we would go back home. We've been saying goodbye to her since we were three and five years old. You'd think we'd be pros at it by now, but we're not; it doesn't get any easier.

Today is Yom Kippur, a day when the traditional wish is, "may your name be inscribed in the book of lives." My mom—the artist who was strong, a little wild, a social bee and a connector—is in the books of many lives. She will be missed but not forgotten.

*   *   *

The morning after Mom passed I didn't want to talk to anyone; I knew they'd be nice to me and that would make me cry. Alan told me that I needed to let people know, but I just couldn't make myself do it. He said it would be okay for me to keep to myself for 24 hours, but then I had to call people and tell them. He called a few of our friends to let them know. I sat on the couch sobbing, where my golden retriever came to find me. She dropped her pink rubber bone in my lap, came in for a snuggle, and then looked at me as if to say, "don't be sad Deb, look—there is so much to play with!"

Coincidentally the first week of Mindfulness Meditation class was one week after Mom had stopped eating. The second class was the week she died. The third class was a couple of days after her Memorial Service. I sat often on my yoga ball, puppy at my feet, sobbing until it was all out, then allowing calm to settle. There were five more classes to go and with each one I was less sad, less tearful, and closer to peace. I maintain that practice still.

A month later, on November 1st, I started to write this book during NaNoWriMo[20]. I had a story to tell and didn't want to hold it in any more. It needed to come out, and I needed to let it. As my wise and brave friend, Sara Pasricha said, "A full life means no holding back."

*   *   *

On November 20th, my Uncle Phil died—on Chip's birthday—but I didn't know until November 22nd. Uncle Phil told me once that the family was perplexed about why my father didn't speak to me for ten years. It touched me deeply; I'd had no idea that anyone felt that way but me. Uncle Phil had a huge and generous heart. Plus, he entrusted me with his top secret pickle recipe—hot and sweet and addictive.

At Uncle Phil's funeral I met Rosie, a childhood friend of Aunt Jean, my father's sister. Rosie knew my mom and said, "You're Sue's daughter, aren't you?" I nodded and smiled, and she

---

[20] National Novel Writing Month – my colleague Linda DeLuca did it in 2009 and I thought it would be a good way for me to develop my writing skills and confidence as a writer. When I sat down at the computer I realized there was much more to it for me than simply being a better writer. www.nanowrimo.org

continued, "I remember her from when we were kids. She was so nice. You look just like her." Pleased and proud, I beamed and replied, "I know she'd love to hear that and I'll be sure to tell her the next time I see her. Thank you!' The conversation continued until about a minute later when I interrupted it, startled and embarrassed, to say, "Oh wait. I'm sorry. I can't tell her. I forgot. She died."

The same day I found out about Uncle Phil's death, I read about grief in Mark Nepo's *The Book of Awakening*. My sister Karen had given it to me after Mom was diagnosed.

In that passage, Nepo wrote "I miss her terribly. And though I resist feeling the loss and emptiness of not having her around, when I lean into that grief, it always in aftermath makes everything more vibrant, more real."

Sometimes I remember my mother or my grandmother and my heart hurts. I get a dull ache from the lump that has formed in my solar plexus, and it reaches up into my throat from the core of me until I choke on it like something stuck there.

He continues, "I've learned that grief can be a slow ache that never seems to stop rising, yet as we grieve, those we love mysteriously become more and more a part of who we are. In this way, grief is yet another song the heart must sing to open the gate of all there is."

I see it this way: sometimes we get to choose what we pack in our bags, and other times we don't. I chose with particular attention and care what to bring with me to Africa and especially up Mt. Kilimanjaro, knowing that I or someone else would be carrying all of the weight of whatever I chose.

Like the core gear for a major climb, my family and life experiences stay with me; I carry them with me throughout my life. But in this case I don't get to choose; they're along for the ride no matter what. Family experiences are written in permanent marker on the notes of my life story. I believe that how I choose to carry them is what forms my character and supports who and how I am as a traveler in this world.

168

In the final paragraph Nepo says, "In truth there is a small one who suffers in each of us, an angel trying to grow wings in the dark, and as this angel learns how to sing, we lose the urge to hide. Indeed, when one heart speaks, all hearts fly. This is what it means to be great—to speak what feels unspeakable and have it release what waits in us all."[21]

Writing this story has helped me find the voice to speak about my whole experience, not just the climb and not just losing Mom, but all of it together. In doing so, it has helped me to release sadness, as well as find forgiveness and acceptance for myself and others.

---

[21] Material excerpted from the book THE BOOK OF AWAKENING ©2000 Mark Nepo with permission from Red Wheel/Weiser, LLC Newburyport, MA and San Francisco, CA www.redwheelweiser.com.

REFLECTION

"The work is off the mountain." -Outward Bound

When I established the desire to climb Mt. Kilimanjaro, I had some non-specific objectives in place about *becoming a lighter presence in the world.* When it was time to climb, I had done some yoga and then not. I didn't lose 20 pounds before I climbed and I only hit my goal to make it to a full, uninterrupted hour on the gauntlet stepping machine at level 6 once; it was boring. I modified the program after having met that goal, skipping around levels 8 and 10 and 12 and with different programs for shorter periods of time (50 minutes, 45 minutes, or 20/30 minutes as part of a circuit). I added in more treadmill work at big inclines and sometimes, on those very sad days, I just jogged or walked and let the tears come. I added in planks and arm exercises with free weights and balancing balls—tips from Coach Amanda. I didn't go caffeine free but I did go without wine for the entire trip with just a few exceptions before and after being on the mountain.

What I discerned, ultimately, is, even a mountain can't hold all your sorrow. She may welcome you, take you to her bosom and soothe your soul, surround you with beauty to delight your senses and remind you of the bigger, timeless world. She may offer challenges to build your spirit, and gentle peace to soothe you for a while, but eventually it's time to go home.

Even a mountain as big as Kilimanjaro can't hold all your sorrow.

BEYOND THE ROOF

You might think that the story would have ended with the accomplishments of crossing the breach, sleeping in the crater, or achieving the summit. You might think that standing on the roof of Africa was the ultimate goal. However, the lessons inspired, born and rooted there live on for me. The impact of the experience came home within me. It wasn't until afterwards—after I came home—after my mother died—after I reflected and wrote about it—that I began to understand what it had taught me.

Wilson was right. *"Don't worry about it."* He'd said. *"Asking the questions now is too soon. The answers will come. When you get home, there will be an entirely different challenge and you don't even know what it is yet."*

That night on the mountain, I knew I'd be facing the challenge of learning how to live without my mother. Unbeknownst to me at the time, there were related challenges. Writing this book, telling this story, has been a challenge for me—it has been the vehicle for me to remember, and feel it again. But this time I have the benefit of reflection. In writing, I immersed myself repeatedly into the tumultuous familial waters, experiencing them as they were before, during and after the climb. And time has provided a safe distance from those waters, allowing me to watch them swirl from the shore this time—a completely different experience

In seeing and experiencing what I did in Africa, I learned important things about myself, about what is important to me and why. I learned how to face my fears, adjust my attitude when necessary and, above all, to try to understand people's past and present behavior and to forgive when I can. I came down from that mountain convinced that patience and polé-polé are keys for me in how I move through this world, in how I want to be.

In seeing and experiencing what I did in Africa, *I know what it feels like to be a lighter presence in the world, because I did it*, and I gained insights about my world that went beyond the roof

171

of Africa: I brought it home with me and it is a part of me forever. I learned more about why I actually did the climb, and what I learned from it, after I came home and started to write this book.

There is a passage often referred to by mountaineers that resonates with me; it was written by René Daumal in his book, *Le Mont Analogue* (originally published in French). The essence of it is this: once a traveler has climbed to the top of a mountain, she *knows* the view from above, and after having descended, the experience is within her. According to Daumal, from that moment, the memory of what the climber has seen informs how she lives, thereafter.

Why did I do this climb? Some crazy, half-baked, unclear idea about being a lighter presence in the world, as though if I lost weight and did yoga and meditated, I would be thin, fabulous and centered, and able to skip up Mt. Kilimanjaro. Maybe I could meditate my way to peace. Maybe I could float up that mountain like a Zen Buddhist.

Why did I do this climb? I went to Africa in search of accomplishing something I could be proud of. The time to leave came in the middle of a family crisis with more gut-wrenching twists than I'd ever experienced simultaneously. The timing of it just happened—the surrounding events, and their synchronicity, were beyond my control. Some may say I was running away from my mom's prognosis and the unpleasant family dynamics that it created and yes, on some level, I was. Not everyone would have chosen to leave her at that time. But Africa called at the same time as the conference and the mountain and the safari. And so I went, and I don't regret it for an instant.

Why did I do this climb? This journey was, for me, about the only thing it could have been at the time: Peace. And Rest. And Comfort for my sadness. It came when I needed distance from my grief, if only for a short while.

Why did I do this climb? Africa is amazingly diverse. I am drawn to her, to this birthplace of humanity. When I close my eyes and imagine Africa, I feel warmth from a setting sun, and see its deep orange light spreading across golden grasses on a plain. I think of the animals that move through it with grace, like the giraffe. I feel the presence of the lioness, the lithe motion of her body and legs as she moves forward with purpose: patient and fearing nothing. I recall old things, prehistoric-looking things like the rhinoceros, and ancient carbon-dated bones—all proof of the age of this place and its timelessness. Listening, I hear the delightful sounds of children at play, "Jambo!" they shout, beckoning me to join them. I hear soulful, spiritual songs sung *a cappella* and in a language you don't have to know to understand because the singers' voices make its meaning clear. Their souls sing to yours. I remember the beauty of the unfolding landscape as it changed from lush, green rainforest, to alpine splendor; and I remember the warm embrace of the vortex there. I sense the "boom" of glaciers and remember their ethereal glow. It is ancient, old and wise, a keeper of time. Grace and wisdom, warmth and comfort—this is how Africa lives with me, in my heart.

*   *   *

Just a few months after my mother was diagnosed, Kevin McCarthy, a friend whose humanity I admire, shared some advice about what he learned after his father died. He stressed to me the importance of dealing with family challenges early, often, and out in the open. If not dealt with, he explained, they'd keep coming back, showing up when you least expect them to, and in ways you may not even recognize. He was so right.

Before I left for Africa, I felt rejected and tossed aside, powerless to do much of anything for Mom and blocked if I tried. I felt like I was on a trapeze, swinging back and forth over a chasm, hanging out there, with no options, and no way to see the next rung to grasp. According to Kevin's advice, that next rung wouldn't appear until I'd dealt with the one I was holding on to.

Living through my African journey forced me to let go of the need to constantly control my world—I had to focus on the mountain, its challenges and its gifts, and let others take care of the rest—especially at home. Here, then, was the essence of the challenge for me—to trust that, while I was on the trapeze, there was a net below me, a net strung with other people's lifelines. If I could loosen my grip enough to have faith in their abilities, and the patience to let things unfold at their own pace—not mine—then the next rung of the trapeze would appear and I could swing on.

Before Mom finished her journey, she made her list of last things to do, and she did all that she could. The only thing left for her was to find peace and to be.

In my journey, I'd hoped for adventure, and peace. But what did I run into? My Self; smacked right into it. All of the planning and research, shopping, packing, the game to make it as light as possible . . . all of that was a way to avoid being alone with my own thoughts, emotions, hurts and faults. While I was busy doing, emotions were oozing out all over the place. For me, this was the push-me-pull-you of being and doing. When being is tough, I look for things to do.

Perhaps the key to my being a lighter presence in the world, especially when my world is in flux, is to do a somersault in mid-air and hang from the trapeze upside down, by the knees. And then . . . to do nothing. Just be.

*   *   *

Writing this story has helped me celebrate and honor, in my own way, a tremendous personal accomplishment. It also helped me realize three things: first, that this time I could handle the altitude; second, that attitude is critical to success; and third, that I can overcome fear.

I acknowledged to myself that I am a serial big goal setter. Making it up and over Kili's Western Breach, then writing and publishing this book, reminded me of what I am capable of. The list of what I learned goes like this . . . .

I learned a new language for living, Swahili-style: *polé-polé* and *hakuna matata.*

I learned that I have stories to tell and that I enjoy the challenge of writing about them.

I learned that I can step right into and through my fear, and find delight on the other side.

I learned that, rather than being like the salmon, I am more like the lioness who is patient and fearing nothing.

I learned that it IS possible for me to let go and allow others to act; that sometimes the best move is none at all.

I learned that I am whole in spite of my fractured past.

I learned that self-confidence starts with self-approval.

I learned that total love, acceptance, and understanding can only come from within.

I learned that life is not always about me.

I learned that every person you meet can teach you something.

I learned that sometimes it's okay to let other people take care of me.

I learned that fear, doubt, guilt and regret are heavy and hard to carry.

I learned that joy, gratitude, acceptance and forgiveness are light and easy to carry.

I learned that in forgiving I became lighter, and life became easier.

I learned that in forgiving others, I released my own burdens, and perhaps theirs, too.

I have chosen to put down the heavy burdens; I placed them, gently, on a leaf and let a calm stream carry them away.

*   *   *

"I haven't been everywhere yet . . . but it's on my list!"

- Susan Sontag

Now people ask, "What's next?," and frankly, I don't know. I'm compelled to figure out what I want to do with this experience before thinking about what's next. It's why I've written this book: to reflect on and share what I experienced, and in writing, editing, reading, editing, editing and editing, to bring clarity for myself, about it all.

My journey in life is certainly not unique; many others face challenges, watch loved ones die, overcome loss and sadness. They, too, grow, remember and continue on.

A client once remarked "I had no idea I was capable of so much change." This has become a motto for me in business, and it's my hope that every one of my clients experiences the same thing. For me, climbing Mt. Kilimanjaro is just one of those big goals I had no idea I was capable of accomplishing. Until I did.

Mt. Kilimanjaro is a long walk up a big and sometimes very steep mountain. It's not a technical climb—I didn't use ropes, pullies, crampons, pins, belays, ladders or any of the equipment a technical climb would require. Many of the Kili climbers I now know are interested in climbing Everest or other technical peaks.

I'll admit it has crossed my mind more than once to attempt such a challenge. Then I realized that, as I joked with my husband, I don't feel the need to do a technical climb because in many ways I've been holding on to the edge for a lot of my life. A different picture is emerging now, that of a confident lioness who is patient and fearing nothing—walking on the edge is where she grows.

Remember.

Trust in your own abilities.

Trust in others' abilities.

All things happen for good

AFTERWORD

I have a photo of my friend and fellow Kili climber, Stan Lee. He is in the center, undoubtedly replenishing his energy with something healthy, surrounded by his family. I met Stan on the airplane home from our separate trekking adventures; it was the last long leg of the journey for us both. I think Stan is a wise old soul in a young man's body and on this flight we talked about animals, great literature and, of course, what it was like to climb Mt. Kilimanjaro. We became friends on Facebook and Stan, the Writer, Philosopher and Triathlete, continues to inspire me and others. I love this photo of Stan and his family of cheerleaders; it was taken after he finished the New York City Marathon.

Do you remember the crazy American students I heard at Lava Tower? While writing this book, Stan reported, "I do have video of me doing 55 pushups at the peak of the Lava Tower, to top the 50 that an Aussie triathlete did moments before me. There was indeed much shouting at the end of my pushup sprint."

If you're considering a climb I would encourage you to do it. As Stan's family reminds us, there's nothin' to it but to do it. And when you do, you become part of this fine club of fellow Kili climbers who, like you, have the mountain in their hearts. I've met some incredibly interesting people in this club—you undoubtedly will too.

*   *   *

It wasn't easy for my husband to let me go to Africa for a month, knowing I may not have been able to contact him, knowing that I would be travelling alone, and knowing that I'd be attempting something challenging and dangerous. We both doubted whether

I was prepared. But he is an amazing man and he would tell you he's married to an amazing woman, and so he let me go. Before I left, he teased me, saying that I needed to go to Africa to "get my mojo back," specifically in the area of gougères, baked cheese puffs that we love. I used to make delicious gougères, but in my experiments with the recipe over several months before leaving for Africa, mine had gone from weird to flat to hockey-puck. I am pleased to report that I do, in fact, have my mojo back and the cheese puffs have been delicious.

*   *   *

I would be remiss not to tell you this part: that I did get to see Dariya again. She emailed to connect early in May 2012, coincidentally, just after I'd met another young woman who would be climbing Mt. Kilimanjaro soon. I invited them both to the house for dinner, and invited Chip too, of course—but I swear this was not a set-up.

We shared an enjoyable evening, talking about adventures all around the world, and about Mt. Kilimanjaro. All along I'd been under the impression that it was Dariya and her group that had camped out in the crater with me that evening. Yes, I thought that they, as nice as they are, were the rude people in the crater, but I was pleased to be wrong. They'd actually started their ascent to the summit, via the crater, in the very early hours of the morning. We talked about the lanky young man who'd had such terrible AMS—they'd seen him too—and about the champagne one of her group brought to the summit.

Together we answered questions for Grace, who would be leaving for her Kilimanjaro adventure in two weeks. I loaned her my Stedman "Encyclopedia," (but only after she promised to bring it back to me), and my inexpensive and unlocked phone-from-Burundi-guaranteed-to-work-in-Tanzania, with instructions to get a new SIM card in Arusha. She also accepted the loan of my yak wool hat with the ear flaps and braided ties, the one that I

180

wished I'd had for my climb; it was from Kathmandu, a gift I received from Alan after I'd come back from Africa. She had everything else she would need and I can't wait to hear all about what it was like for her.

*   *   *

I reached the summit of Mt. Kilimanjaro on June 20, 2011.

Once I realized it might actually be possible to publish my story, not surprisingly, I set a goal for publication. It seemed obvious to me: this book should be published on the one year anniversary of my summit: June 20, 2012.

In doing research for this book I was not entirely surprised to learn that my summit date has broader meaning. June 20th is Africa Refugee Day. In 2001 the United Nations declared it World Refugee Day.

*   *   *

Twice in my life so far my dreams have offered the comfort of closure after a broken heart. The first was after a breakup. Here is the story of the second, which happened after months of working on this book.

I woke up from a dream on a May morning several months after Mom died; it was just a few days after her birthday. In the dream there were people wearing long, white robes with beaded fronts— thousands of white and ivory bugle beads sewn in a vertical pattern several inches wide across the bodice, and reaching down to a wide, cathedral point just below mid-body. The beading shimmered like light on water.

The women who caught my attention wore silver hats with wide, coin-shaped petals on them like an old-fashioned bathing cap; the silver petals fluttered gently in the soft breeze. All of the people were smiling and waving in a relaxed way, and looking off to my right.

The people were standing on tiered personal balconies, like something you'd see on a cruise ship. The ship was white and clean, with minimally tasteful dark blue trim, and the railings each person held with one hand were gleaming, polished silver.

Two young women turned to smile at me. I couldn't see details of their faces; rather I sensed and caught only the briefest moment of focus on bright eyes and happy smiles. One face was surrounded by soft brunette curls, the other blond.

In the moment the two women looked at me; I knew that one was my mother and one was her mother, my grandmother.

I woke up and realized it was a dream.

Throughout the day, I thought about what the dream might mean. It accompanied me as I went through a morning routine: fed the dog, got the papers and made coffee. I rolled it around in my mind throughout the day.

Perhaps it was my subconscious telling me that she was okay and that it was time for me to let my sadness sail away. It was May 13th. It was Mother's Day.

THE TITLE OF THIS BOOK

Over dinner one recent evening Alan and I were discussing the working title of the book. I was explaining my resistance to my own first idea of calling it "My" Kilimanjaro, since I don't think an experience like this is anything that can be owned by a person. Rather it becomes a part of you and stays with you always, as do many experiences over a lifetime. I think to own it exclusively isn't possible; it goes against laws of nature. Who can hold the whole mountain?

After listening, Alan offered his perspective. To him, this was the story of one woman's solo summit. It was an "aha" moment for me. I hadn't considered it from that angle, which will probably surprise those who know me since I admire stories of barrier-breakers, especially about strong women who break through them. I love championing the underdog, cheering and celebrating with pride those who are brave enough to challenge the system, question the status quo. How odd then, that I wasn't thinking of this as a solo female adventure.

He's right, of course, that I did go it alone in one sense, but that's mostly because I couldn't get anyone to come with me! "That's your dream, Deb," Alan would remark when I'd ask him if he wanted to come.

It's not like I set out to make it a solo adventure, it just turned out that way. I was always open to the possibility of climbing with others. The folks at SENE knew that I was open to joining a group or welcoming others to join with me on the dates I was available to climb, and besides, it's less expensive to travel in a group. My schedule just didn't mesh with anyone else's though, and so it was just me.

Actually, it was me and a team of ten men. Porters, chefs, guides, all of which I thought was extreme for just one client. Being the independent, DIY person I am, I was embarrassed that anyone thought I needed the help of ten people. I knew from my reading that there would be a team, since it is required by law, but ten men? Puh-lease! Then I learned it wasn't a comment on my abilities as a woman or as a solo or anything. It wasn't about me at all—it's the minimum number this company has on any team, no exceptions. Honest explained it to me this way, he said, "Deb, because you are here and we are working, our families will have nice things."

"Okay," I said, "Ten men it is."

Even if it were possible to climb solo, I still couldn't call this a solo journey because I believe that we are never alone. It may feel that way sometimes, but even a hermit living in a cave interacts with a living environment. "If a tree falls in the forest and there is no person there to hear it, does it make a sound?" How would you answer this kōan[22]?

I think there is just one answer. To me, the answer is yes—it absolutely does make a sound. There is life everywhere in the forest and even if there are no creatures with ears to hear it, what is sound but vibration? Sound can be felt. Creaky old man glaciers announce their presence, they wake up to each day whether I am the one sleeping in the crater or not. So, yes, I believe that the tree falling in the forest is heard even if there is no person there to hear it. We exist. Others exist. The planet is living. Therefore, we are never alone.

This reminds me of the African philosophy of Ubuntu, which describes what is to me a truly wonderful way of being in the world. A person with Ubuntu is generous and caring; they use their strengths on behalf of others and in that sharing, their humanity is inextricably intertwined. Desmond Tutu says, "A person is a person through other people." We are born from other humans, we learn what we know from others and in this way, "we need other human beings in order to be human. The solitary, isolated human being is a contradiction in terms."[23]

---

[22] A kōan is a paradoxical question designed to inspire thoughtful contemplation.

[23] From *Believe——The Words and Inspiration of Desmond Tutu*

None of us walks the path alone—great things happen from the power of the community. That's probably why I didn't think of this as one woman's journey, it's just another thing I wanted to do and so I did it.

What would you do if you were not afraid?

The results may surprise you.

MY KILIMANJARO "REPORT CARD"

The previous "report card" example provided data only up to and including Lava Tower. The datasheet below includes every day on the mountain.

Client Vitals Sheet for Deb Denis, Female, Age 46, Height: 5', 6"
Weight: *Nope, I'm still not putting that in here.*

		Elevation (Feet)	O2 Saturation (%)	Heart Rate (BPM)	Respiration breath/min	Water Intake (litres)	Diamox 250mgx2	Location	Other
11-Jun-11	AM	6000	95	70	9			Mbahe Farm	
11-Jun-11	PM	6000	96	73	8			Mbahe Farm	
12-Jun-11	AM	6000	96	84	9		x	Mbahe Farm	
12-Jun-11	PM	5800	97	76	8	2	x	Simba Farm	
13-Jun-11	AM	5800	95	70	7.5		x	Simba Farm	
13-Jun-11	PM	8700	92	79	8	2.5	x	Big Tree Camp	
14-Jun-11	AM	8700	93	78	8		x	Big Tree Camp	
14-Jun-11	PM	11420	89	74	7	3	x	Shira 1	light headache; naproxen x2
15-Jun-11	AM	11420	87	72	8		x	Shira 1	
15-Jun-11	PM	12750	88	72	7	3	x	Shira 2	
16-Jun-11	AM	12750	90	77	8.5		x	Shira 2	
16-Jun-11	PM	15230	85	81	9	3.5	x	Lava Tower	light headache; naproxen x2
17-Jun-11	AM	15230	85	74	8		x	Lava Tower	
17-Jun-11	PM	15230	87	77	10	3	x	Lava Tower	
18-Jun-11	AM	15230	88	78	9		x	Lava Tower	
18-Jun-11	PM	15980	84	77	8	3	x	Arrow Glacier	
19-Jun-11	AM	15980	78	88	11		x	Arrow Glacier	
19-Jun-11	PM	18800	69	97	10	2.5	x	Crater	headache; naproxen ineffective
20-Jun-11	AM	18800	68	95	11			Crater	puffy eyes, face
20-Jun-11	PM	12530	91	79	8	2		Millenium Camp	
21-Jun-11	AM	12530	90	67	8.5			Millenium Camp	

ACKNOWLEDGMENTS

Thanks to my family. To my sister, Karen, who always believes in me, no matter what. We'll always be okay as long as we have each other . . . and plenty of snacks. And to Alan, Chip and Mike—you have no idea how much I wanted you to be with me—I appreciate your support and the training, since climbing mountains as a family helped me prepare, on so many levels, for this adventure.

To Mom, who let me go. To my other sisters and brothers (in-laws included here) who step to the plate in life—I think you are amazing, resilient and strong. To my beautiful nephews, Colin, Trey and Georgie-the-butterfly-man whose way of being is pure and whose art work came with me to Africa; I know that someday we will go to Peru.

Thanks to Dad for kicking me out of the nest; it builds character. To Uncle Don, Kit, Danny and Chris, my cousin who wore a parka when he worked atop Mauna Kea in Hawaii, who we lost much, much too soon in 2011. To Aunt Jean and Uncle Phil, whose empathy and kindness touched my heart deeply. To Norma and Joe for unconditional love and support, and for the ISBN for this book.

Thanks especially to three Linda's, inspirational writers all . . .

To Linda DeLuca: You are an inspirational teacher and I love discovering and learning from and with you. We may be "independents" in the working world, but you are with me every day, and together, we are brilliant.

To my business partner in The Athena Project, Linda Pennington, who shares her very generous heart and considerable wisdom, and in doing so, helps me build mine. You brought the coaching style to your work as an Editor of this book and what a difference it made. We are the power of 2.

To Linda C. Hamilton, Editor of this book, practicing attorney, adjunct writing instructor and beautifully lyric writer, who read the first copy of this book, which was an awful mess. When you said, "You have something here," you gave me hope. It may never have made it out into the world if not for you. You inspire me, and have taught me so much about writing through this project. I am grateful to infinity and beyond, for you.

Thanks must go to those who were kind enough to share their own experiences with me including Henry Stedman, You Tube guy LDGarber. Amanda Downs, Rhonda Evans, and Matt Friedman. Thanks to Stig Nygaard for letting me use his photo, and to Dariya and team for sharing their adventure. Thanks also to other SENE climbers, especially Linda Till, who all provided authentic feedback on their experience with SENE. Thanks to Jolene Wilson-Glah for walk and talks—I know you'll make it and I can't wait to hear all about it after you do.

Thanks to the SENE crew who took such commendable care of me from pre-decision to post-trip, especially to Tim Leinbach, one of the most patient people in the world since he answers the same questions time after time with the same love and care. And I can't forget *Watu Azuri* (the Best Team): guides Honest Matto and Wilson Moshe, my entire crew, the staff at Mbahe and at HQ in Moshi.

Simon Mtuy, you have honored me with the Foreword to this book. You honor your country by being a stellar ambassador. You honor your clients, through SENE, by helping each of them achieve a dream. Thank you.

Thanks to the folks at CA who brought me over to work with them and in doing so taught me about Africa and more, especially, thanks to Heidrun Kippenberger—I want to know you until we're both very old.

Thanks to the many friends, mentors and teachers who have helped me along the way, some of whom are mentioned in the telling of this story.

And to those early readers, who were generous with their time to read and provide feedback and ideas. I am most grateful for your encouragement to tell more of my inner story. And to Lisa Presson, the last preprint reader, for seeing what I could not.

Thanks to you, Dear Reader, and to every client and friend and person I don't even know who listens to me tell stories from the mountain because it's a gift that refreshes my soul each time. I hope it inspires yours.

Dear Reader,

The story part of the book ends here.

The next section contains my notes from planning and packing. It includes details of how I made the decisions regarding what to bring and what not to bring and why, which company to climb with and why.

This next section is valuable for anyone planning to climb but it may be considerably less interesting for those who aren't actually making the trek.

Thank you for travelling with me,

Deb

APPENDIX: RESEARCH, EQUIPMENT, PACK LIST

"Ain't nothin to it, but to do it"
Writer, Philosopher and fellow Kili climber, Stanley Lee

This section of the book is included for all of the people who are considering or preparing for a Kilimanjaro adventure. It includes all of my notes and then some on what to bring and what to consider when you're planning your adventure. I found some terrific resources that should be shared; that's why they're here. Take each with a grain of salt, as I did, using what is most important for your own preparation.

The best piece of advice I can offer, something I was told by three different people on three separate occasions immediately before I left for Tanzania is this: *Have fun with it!*

RESEARCH, RESEARCH, RESEARCH

A lot of people want to know about the research so I'm sharing it here. My research included online, print and personal references. I read reviews, blogs, looked at other people's pictures and talked about it with people I knew and didn't know. I used tools from my own Coaching toolkit, like Lewin's Forcefield Analysis, which helped me narrow down key areas of focus—specifically it helped me to be very clear on what might get in my way. I engaged a sport coach in Canada. I asked personal trainers at my gym and even one former Trainer-turned-Accountant who was in my home for dinner, for advice on how to prepare.

I went to two favorite sources: Google and Amazon. From Amazon, I bought a few used books and one new copy of Henry Stedman's book, *Kilimanjaro—a trekking guide to Africa's highest mountain*, which I proceeded to devour and study, reading it at night before going to bed, with a pen in hand for notes and a highlighter for items to research further. Stedman's Trekking guide gives you an idea of what's possible—from there it is up to you to choose and design your ultimate adventure. It's all possible.

I'd say the Stedman book is required reading and bring it with you because it describes the trails in detail; I read it most nights on the mountain before falling asleep, so I could see what to expect the next day for terrain and climate. Stedman gives the reader a ton of unbiased, well-researched information on everything you need to think about and then some. Without a doubt, it is a bible for the Kili climber in my opinion.

There are SO many choices for guide services and though Stedman provides reviews of many of them, he's right when he also tells you he's just tipping the iceberg of options; a quick search on Google will confirm that there are many more guide services out there. I did look into a few that I found on Google and when I couldn't get information on them in Stedman's book, I'd ask questions—posting them online and asking other tour operators over the phone. I even emailed Henry Stedman, who provided info where he could.

I worked with Amanda Downs (awdcoaching.com—her motto is "Let's get moving!") who recommended that I speak with a friend of hers, Ronda Evans, who'd just completed the climb with her husband to celebrate their wedding anniversary. Ronda provided pictures and video that made it seem more possible to me and I'm so very grateful for that encouragement. Although she's my age, Ronda is a soccer player and coach, and she runs a women's soccer league, so I knew I couldn't slack on the physical preparation for this challenge.

I read the reviews and blogs of other Kili climbers who wrote about their experience—I think it's time for me to contribute to that body of knowledge too. Though I haven't done it online (yet), I have served as an unofficial ambassador for the company I eventually chose, telling anyone who wants to know about my experience, no matter which company they decide to go with.

I've spoken to a few people who are considering the climb with SENE and I can't say enough about how pleased I was with that decision.

There were far too many options on the Internet to get a good sense of criteria for narrowing the search, and I needed to find some way to narrow it down so that I could identify what would make it the very best experience for me. I was looking at what I consider to be a very serious amount of money but even more so, I wanted to know as much as possible, to prepare as much as possible, so that I could make the summit.

If there was to be any obstacle I couldn't overcome, I felt I needed to identify it sooner rather than later and get to work on it. Stedman's guide doesn't rank one route over another, one service over another, rather he provides data to inform *your* choice—I liked that. The information helped me narrow down the choices that were most attractive *to me.*

DECIDING WHICH ROUTE TO TAKE

Some of this first part is a slight repeat from what's in an earlier chapter of the book. Here you get all of my thoughts on it in this longer version of how I determined which route to take and why.

One route was labeled as dangerous in comparison to others. Less than ten percent of Kilimanjaro climbers choose the Western Breach route, also referred to as the Lemosho Crater route, but it was the one that sparkled most with interesting facets for me. Unlike any other, on the Western Breach route you get to sleep in the crater of the volcano at 18,800 feet. There is the possibility to feel the ground warm to the touch. The volcanic dust is soft to sleep in. There are glaciers! Yes, it was dangerous, but the idea of sleeping in the crater was irresistible to me. This was my route for sure.

Another big attraction of this route: sleeping in the crater puts you just 90 minutes away from the summit the next morning, a gift when you consider that on the other routes trekkers have to wake up in the middle of the night in order to make it to the summit and back down all in one day. I wanted to enjoy the summit, not to be wiped out getting there; it seemed to me the 90 minute trek was the best since I in fact did not know how I'd respond to the altitude.

Here is how SENE describes it in their summary of the Lemosho Crater Route: *"This is our most popular itinerary for its beauty, 9 total days on the mountain (for maximum acclimatization), and the excitement of spending an overnight at 18,800 feet inside the crater on Kilimanjaro. The route takes us from the west across the Shira Plateau, with an ascent to the base of the Lava Tower, which you will be able to climb for magnificent 360 degree vistas. From Lava Tower there are two approaches to the crater and summit. Groups will have discussed and decided upon their choice during their climb preparations in Mbahe. One approach is from the southwest through the Western Breach, the classic route to the crater with a challenging rock scramble done in the early morning. The other is a longer and less steep approach from Barafu, farther east, and offering the opportunity of summiting twice. After the overnight camped in the soft sand of the crater, we have a sunrise climb to Uhuru Peak before descending toward the southeast and incredible views of Mawenzi, Kilimanjaro's remnant volcanic cone."*

Sorry I can't offer too many videos of my own about the breach because it was too steep for me to do much of anything with my camera. I took this part of the trip VERY SERIOUSLY and the camera stayed tucked into the inner pocket of my jacket to protect it from freezing, defrosting, or getting smashed. But I did find this link, and if you're interested in taking this route, check out these videos to get a feel for it: http://wn.com/Western_Breach

The altitude is what intimidated me the most. Yes, I was (and still am) out of top shape, but my legs are strong and I've been hiking with my husband and our sons for the ten years we've been a family, so I believed that I had the physical strength to do it. In my opinion, it was altitude and attitude that were most likely to be my obstacles.

As you read in the story, I've been dizzy on fast ascents before—flying into Aspen, CO and driving over Independence Pass (12,095ft/3687m) I got the dizzies big time, and again on the Matterhorn (3885m/12,780ft) despite a week of acclimatization in Zermatt. So, my history was dizziness at more than 12,000 feet, and I was contemplating climbing to 19,340 feet. Could I do it? Altitude and attitude were the only obstacles I thought might be in my way.

I wanted to give myself every advantage possible within reason. Research told me that the more time on the trail, the better to acclimatize. The longer the trek, the more likely I was to adapt to the climate; Independence Pass in Aspen and the Matterhorn were both dizziness after rapid ascents by car and ski lift, whereas Kilimanjaro would be en pied, on foot: walking in. Add that to the list: preference for Western Breach, crater camping and as long a trek as reasonably possible. These became my top criteria for evaluating each option.

DECIDING WHEN TO CLIMB

There were additional criteria: first that the timing had to coincide with the work in Burundi, which was my priority.

Would I climb before Burundi or after? I decided that climbing after Burundi would be best—what if I was hurt on the climb and unable to meet my commitment to Heidrun? Plus, I was looking forward to this conference and wanted to do the work first, do an exceptional job with it, and then play.

Second, Stedman's book talked about the preference of climbers to summit on a full moon and so that came into play too. I think that if you're taking a traditional summit that involves climbing between midnight and pre-sunrise hours of the morning, then a full moon could be advantageous, but for me, and for anyone else taking the western breach, I think you don't need to concern yourself with this as a decision-making criterion because you're never walking at night. Plus, the full moon is so very bright at that altitude that it obscures a lot of the stars in the night sky. As schedules would have it, I would not be summiting on a full moon. It would, however, fill up the sky on my way up and I can tell you with full certainty that bright a June full moon will always remind me of my time on Mt. Kilimanjaro.

CORE VALUES – USE WHAT'S MOST IMPORTANT TO YOU

Another criterion came not from nice to have or even need to have but from a deeper place, from my core values. Studying at the University of Pennsylvania (UPenn) I discovered a treasuretrove of a website full of interesting assessments being developed by the folks in the Positive Psychology department. One in particular was influential in my research into what I believe to be essential in coaching: knowing and living by your values.

The website is www.authentichappiness.com and my favorite assessment there is the Values In Action (VIA) Strengths Questionnaire. Decades of global research by Positive Psychologists identified 24 character strengths and virtues common among all people, all around the world. They call these 'values in action' and the results of the self-assessment rank their importance to you. My top five, from the long version of the questionnaire, are:

Your Top Strength—Fairness, equity, and justice

Treating all people fairly is one of your abiding principles. You do not let your personal feelings bias your decisions about other people. You give everyone a chance.

Your Second Strength—Gratitude

You are aware of the good things that happen to you, and you never take them for granted. Your friends and family members know that you are a grateful person because you always take the time to express your thanks.

Your Third Strength—Capacity to love and be loved

You value close relations with others, in particular those in which sharing and caring are reciprocated. The people to whom you feel most close are the same people who feel most close to you.

Your Fourth Strength—Forgiveness and mercy

You forgive those who have done you wrong. You always give people a second chance. Your guiding principle is mercy and not revenge.

Your Fifth Strength—Curiosity and interest in the world

You are curious about everything. You are always asking questions, and you find all subjects and topics fascinating. You like exploration and discovery.

I encourage you to take the VIA assessment for yourself. You'll have to register on the site but I know from personal experience that they won't spam you based on that registration. In fact, your data will contribute to an ever-increasing global body of knowledge used by scholars around the world, and that's a nice way to pay it forward, isn't it? You'll find lots of interesting and free assessments there—have fun with it!

I read about the life of the porters on Mt. Kilimanjaro, specifically about how companies mistreat them and knew, based on my #1 VIA—a strong sense of fairness, equity and justice— that I had to bring my business to a company that treated its porters well. The Kilimanjaro Porter's Assistance Project (KPAP) was formed to ensure fair treatment; they are committed to improving the working conditions of the porters on

Kilimanjaro and I wanted my money to go to a company that was a member of KPAP.

HEALTH CONSIDERATIONS

I've spoken to many people during their research stage and have heard from women who struggle with Fibromyalgia, arthritis, cancer and its treatments: chemotherapy and radiation, yet they still consider the climb. Their determination and strength amaze me.

I consider myself healthy, but I do have one health challenge that's a nuisance more than anything and I mention it here in case you have the same. I have sleep apnea and use a CPAP every night. Now how would THAT fit into my month in Africa?

Treating it like the practical consideration it is, I looked into and considered several options. There are no power plugs on the mountain. Rechargeable battery packs may or may not last long enough, were quite heavy and they were expensive. I called my doctor for advice and found out about a nasal patch, fairly new to market, which I ordered with her prescription. The sample pack was affordable enough and I was able to try them before I left, as she suggested. The patch seemed to do the trick well enough, though application and breathing through it took some getting used to, and this became my option. Nice, huh? I do believe that we get what we need when we need it.

There was just one problem: the adhesive is uber sticky and left booger-looking residue on my nose after pulling it off in the morning. The worst part: removing it each morning was like pulling off a Band-Aid that had been super glued to my nose. When my nose hit maximum sunburn level, both the 'rip it off' and 'gentle, gentle, gentle' approaches hurt like hell and brought tears to my eyes. Still, it's better than carrying a CPAP and there was no one the in my tent to complain to, so I determined to suck it up and, as the Pennsylvania Dutch would say, "kwitchyerbellyakin."

Vitamins and meds were another consideration. I brought my regular daily multi and fish oil. I added chlorophyll—for improved oxygenation—to my vitamin mix after reading that many people who live at altitude take it regularly. I figured it couldn't hurt and even started taking it at home to boost the effectiveness of my workouts. I still take it.

I brought and used electrolyte tablets in my water bottle a few days, just for a change up. They were recommended by my son, Chip, an avid outdoorsman, and REI had them in orange-ginger and berry flavors which were delicious.

I would be taking anti-malarial drugs the whole time—strongly recommended due to my visits to Burundi and the Serengeti— and had to choose my pain medicine carefully as a result, to avoid drug interactions. My research indicated an NSAID would be best and I chose Naproxen Sodium because I take it for sore muscles and am familiar with how it works for me.

At the time of my travel there were three choices for prophylactic anti-malarial treatment. The oldest and least expensive pill had an unusual side-effect: hallucinations. Susan at UPenn Travel Medicine thought it best not to fiddle with possible hallucinations while climbing a steep mountain and I agreed!

The newest and best option was $8 a pill, even if I ordered it from Canada, and I needed sixty pills so THAT wasn't my favorite option. The middle of the road pill had given some people stomach problems so Susan suggested I take it for a few days at home first, and then decide. The generic version of this last option was about $13 for the whole 60 day supply, which didn't bother my wallet, and fortunately it didn't bother my stomach either. Like Goldilocks, I thought this one was just right.

Rounding out the med pack were small packets of anti-bacterial ointment, Tiger Balm and Traumeel for sore muscles if needed, and Cortizone cream for itch or rash if needed. Band-Aids and Second Skin patches for blisters, with a tiny roll of duct tape as back up. UPenn Travel Medicine recommended pills for antidiarrhea as well as generic Cipro, both of which I brought but thankfully did not need.

PAPERWORK

Penn Travel Medicine was a superb resource. They knew what was required, what was 'optional' and helped me decide on boosters, shots and pills. They provided exactly the information I might need to consider, like water purification and travel health insurance.

I flip-flopped about buying travel insurance, then decided the few hundred dollars that it would cost for this journey were worth the peace of mind that comes from having a safety net. I'd read that helicopter rescues could run about US$8,000 and would require cash. I didn't have that much cash and even if I did, I wouldn't be carrying it with me. No, insurance was a better way to go, so I splurged. Thankfully Murphy's Law kicked in and I didn't need to use it.

I didn't need a travel visa for Tanzania, but did need one for Burundi and also for Kenya[24], where a visa is required even to fly through the airport. I found conflicting information on whether or not these visas could be purchased on the spot or were needed in advance; I wasn't taking any chances and mailed my passport to the embassies in Washington, DC to get what I needed. My passport included an updated 'yellow card' with proof of that all my shots were up-to-date.

I registered my full itinerary with the U.S. Department of State, as mentioned in the story, thanks to the prompting of my very experienced international travelling husband. The website:

---

[24] Check on visa requirements before you travel, of course. As of the writing of this book (one year from my travel there), I confirmed that a travel visa IS required for Tanzania and that one is NOT required for travel via Kenya if you stay in the international terminal of the airport.

travel.state.gov is an excellent resource to check, and register with, as you plan and before you travel.

TRAINING FOR KILI, SOMEONE ELSE'S NOTES

My friend Linda DeLuca sent me some valuable links during the planning process. The pieces that I found especially helpful were compiled and saved with my planning notes; I offer it here in case you may find it helpful too. Please excuse any repetition with the other notes.

You should start training for climbing Kilimanjaro at least two months prior to your departure. If you've never hiked before, you should start with shorter time intervals, a slower pace, and no weight (in your day pack) and then gradually increase all of the above as your fitness level improves. Remember that on Mount Kilimanjaro, you will walk slowly for prolonged periods, and carry probably no more than 20 lbs. in your day pack. Therefore, in your training, it is better to increase the time interval/distance and keep a slow pace than to shorten the time interval/distance and increase the pace. Try to train three times a week, for at least one hour per session, at a minimum. If you can do day hikes for four to six hours, with moderate elevation changes (~1,500 ft/460 m) while carrying a 20 pound pack, or if you can walk on a stairmaster for one to two hours, at 30 steps per minute while carrying a 20 pound pack, then you're probably ready for the real thing.

Your longest/hardest workouts should be performed two to four weeks before your departure. For the last two weeks, you should taper off your training and in the final days, rest so that your body has time to recover before your actual climb. In addition to walking/hiking, you can also supplement your training with exercises such as running or cycling, which will increase your aerobic capacity.

It is imperative that during Kilimanjaro training, you wear the boots that you intend to climb with so that they are sufficiently broken-in (to prevent blisters). Additionally, you should wear the day pack you intend to carry so you're your shoulders/back/hips get used to the points of contact and weight (to minimize chafing and soreness).

Lastly, physical training is just one part of getting in shape. If you have an unhealthy lifestyle, use the climb as your motivation to change. Eat more fruits and vegetables. Reduce your red meat consumption. Don't drink or smoke. Get eight hours of sleep per night. Don't worry. Be happy.

Sources (from Linda D)

http://www.ultimatekilimanjaro.com/preparation.htm
http://www.davestravelcorner.com/journals/publish/article_21.shtml

COST $, $$, OR $$$ AND THEN SOME

Cost would be a consideration since I saw wildly different numbers depending on routes, days, hotels, food, equipment, and the list goes on. I didn't want to get into a negotiation and in each inquiry asked for inclusive rates. Companies that responded with too many 'optional' items didn't make the cut. This is, of course, a personal preference—as are all of these criteria.

I met a group on the mountain that was looking for exactly the opposite; they wanted no frills, low cost and a fast ascent. I saw them at Millennium camp on the way down, where they had been without food for about a day due to miscommunication between their guides and porters and them. I learned when I came back and read their blog that they were the ones who had lost one of their guides in the middle of the night due to altitude sickness. You can read about the terrific adventures of this group of four twenty-something Russian-American adventurers here: www.wegoingup.com.

I knew none of their experience at the time I was making decisions, of course, but I knew clearly this was not the trip for me to go no frills.

Maybe if I were a twenty-something I would have considered it, but something this adventurous wouldn't have entered the conceivable realm of possibilities to me in my 20s—I'm a late blooming outdoor adventurer.

My criteria for selection then were:

1. The start date—had to be right after the conference in Burundi

2. The route—had to be via the Western Breach—Lemosho Crater

3. The length of time—had to be long to aid in acclimatization

4. The company—had to be a member of KPAP

5. The cost—had to be fully inclusive

Narrowing it Down

I created a spreadsheet of the 16 companies that looked good based on the research up to this point. Now, to narrow it down. I contacted each company via VOIP (Skype) or email and in each inquiry provided my hard start date and desired route. Would they start on my date? Do they offer the route I want up the western breach? Some companies were more responsive than others. Those that responded remained on the list.

The list narrowed to ten companies, which I continually ranked and sorted based on incoming available data. Ashante, Shidolya Tours, Kiliwarriors, Marangu Hotel, Stedman's own company Climb Mount Kilimanjaro, and Peter Tours & Mountaineering. I appreciated talking with Carol at Kiliwarriors and though our dates weren't simpatico, I would recommend anyone considering a climb give them a serious look because I appreciated her level of responsiveness and candor; she was willing to spend time talking with me even after it became clear I wouldn't be going with them since the dates didn't match. Same for Stedman's company, where the mismatch was on the route.

My dates and desired route proved to be a very quick way to narrow it down. Many of the ten were taking groups only, which would not have been a problem except that the group climbs were timed to coincide with a full moon summit and there weren't that many in a row since we were just before the busy season which begins in June, when it is winter in Africa. My dates were *just* beyond most of the pre-arranged groups, literally by a couple of days.

Many of the ten didn't take the western breach/Lemosho Crater route at all. Remember the dangerous part? Well, Tanzanian officials closed that route for several years after a serious avalanche killed 3 climbers and another took out one of the camps. People have died on this route in rock slides and avalanches. Still, I was undeterred . . . many people had made it up that route after all, yet I found the majority of companies wouldn't even consider taking clients up the western breach. That's okay—it helped me to narrow the list to three levels.

On the third level was the DikDik hotel. They were attractive with gourmet meals and looking quite posh, plus they're used by Rainier Mountain Guides, a well-respected US-based climbing company. And I do like good food . . . .

I can't resist sharing this story with you: A dikdik is the smallest gazelle, about the size of a tiny toy dog. I knew my nephews would giggle at the name, they're little boys after all, and so I made a point of capturing one on video in the Serengeti. As luck would have it, this little dikdik had to do his business just at that moment, dropping little pellets, then back-kicking dirt over them to cover. I caught it all in on video and couldn't wait to bring to my nephews this video of a dikdik pooping—I would definitely be the coolest Ant Deb.

On level two was Zara Tours owned by "Mama Zara," attractive to me because it's a woman-owned company. Also on level 2 was Peak Planet, who uses African Walking Tours on the ground in-country. Zara Tours was inexpensive and I wondered how they were able to keep the costs so low. Feedback I'd received indicated that Zara Tours is considered the Costco of Kili tours, one person thought it "too big for a personal experience" and thought other operators offered better lodging/location. Again, it's all what's important to you for your adventure.

Two companies made level one: Premier Tours, who would be using Wild Frontiers in-country. I like Premier Tours a lot because Julian, our local expert on African travel, arranged a once-in-a-lifetime experience for Alan and me in South Africa a few years ago. I loved that adventure and Premier Tours had something no other company on my list had: they are a known entity to my husband, who would be much more comfortable with my selection if it were Julian and Premier Tours. This was strongly in their favor since Alan was less than ecstatic about the idea of his wife travelling around East Africa solo. The other #1 choice was SENE whose American representative, Tim Leinbach, was incredibly responsive.

I shared little of this with Alan while the research was in progress, for a couple of reasons. First, because he was nervous about my solo travel to what he thought could be dangerous places. For months, he cut out newspaper stories of safari travelers who'd been abducted, held for ransom and murdered in the Serengeti, Kenya, and West Africa. Second, he would not be coming with me. Not for lack of offering—I asked him on a regular basis if he would consider coming with me, even just meeting up for safari after the climb—but he was travelling for business to both Mexico before and China during my dates. Also, neither of us was ready to believe that it would actually happen until the dates for the conference in Burundi were set in stone and I knew with certainty that I'd be going.

To help me decide, SENE offered the email addresses and names of eight of their clients. I emailed then all:

> *Hello, my name is Deb and I'm about ready to*
> *sign the agreement with SENE to take me up*

Kili—Lemosho/Western Breach—as a solo traveler. I'd really like to know—of all the companies out there (and there are SO many!), why did you choose SENE? If you had it to do all over again, would you change anything about your climb? I'd be most appreciative of your advice and perspective—please share it all in an email, or let's set up a time to chat via Skype.

I was surprised by the responses. Each and every person I wrote to responded, offering not just a quick "oh, they were good" answer, but instead providing paragraphs of remembrance and ideas, links to blogs and photo albums, their notes were filled with glowing recommendations. What a generous and interesting community of people I was meeting on this inquiry alone!

From the women in particular I wanted to know if they considered it safe enough for a woman travelling alone and I was assured that it would not be an issue at all. I spoke with two women on the phone—I had so many questions and wanted to know what it was like. One of these dynamos is Linda Till, who offered invaluable advice on how to prepare, what to expect, and encouragement. She even offered to lend me clothing if I needed any gear, which was incredibly generous. But she's a size 2 and I'm a 14. In hindsight, I should have borrowed her gloves because mine were inadequate!

While doing this research, I was waiting as patiently as possible for Heidrun to give me the go ahead to book my flights. It's my personal preference in situations like this to plan as much as possible in advance—within what I consider reasonable at least. I prefer having reservations for the big ticket items like flights, hotels, car as needed, set.

On this trip, the big ticket items to pre-arrange and pay for were the flights and the guide company since Heidrun's organization would cover everything in-country in Burundi, and I would only go with a climbing company that would take care of all transportation, including hotel and airport transfers (so no worries about renting a car or taking long taxi rides).

I wanted it all arranged in advance so there would be less to worry about during the travel. I know from experience that schedules and plans can sometimes change without notice when you're travelling.

When Heidrun finally confirmed that the dates had stopped moving and were set, I got into motion to shore up the arrangements.

And the Winner is . . . .

Tim Leinbach, the SENE representative in the U.S., spent about 45 minutes on the phone with me, answering questions as I did my research. In the end, it was the high touch that made the difference for me. Though they were in the higher end, bottom-line pricewise, to me there was clearly very high value for that money. 13 days including acclimatization on an organic Chagga farm on the mountain sounded idyllic, cleansing and delicious (and it was). Exposure to the culture and a very personal connection—the farm is owned by Simon Mtuy, who runs SENE and was the original record holder for fastest supported ascent/descent of the mountain, running both up and down on December 26, 2004. In fact, the round trip for Simon was 8 hours 27 minutes—six hours to reach the summit (took me seven days) and after seven minutes to catch his breath, just two hours twenty minutes to descend (took me two days). This record, for a "supported" climb, has since been bested; however, Simon Mtuy remains the world record holder for the fastest unsupported ascent and descent of Mt. Kilimanjaro of 9 hours, 22 minutes.

SENE is 100% Tanzanian owned. They are one of the biggest supporters of KPAP. And, uniquely, they specialize in the Western Breach route. What also set them apart was a willingness to arrange a private trek—many of the other companies were only able to include me in groups already set to go, which makes complete sense to me from a business operations standpoint.

High touch, very personalized service, an extended and unique stay for acclimatization and culture and good, fresh, organic food, first-rate reputation and specializing in my chosen route—I was confident in my selection and put the contract in motion.

I appreciated the 56-page *Mambo Mbalimbali* (Swahili for "Various Things") that answers almost every question a prospective climber may have, and others the prospective climber may not even think of. What to expect, how to prepare, photos—I thought it was a wise and thorough approach to educate, welcome and prepare clients. I appreciated that there were very few things not included and that made it so much easier for me.

With the Big Decision made, I could enjoy leisure reading. I read Ernest Hemingway's *Snows of Kilimanjaro*, of course. I've always admired Hemingway's style of writing; he shows just the tip of the iceberg, just the surface, but with enough clues to the significant story beneath the surface, which he leaves to your imagination. As a writer, he could give the reader all of the answers but he chose instead to let the reader ponder and discover their own perspectives on the story based on his carefully chosen words in deep, rich, colorful, minimalist style. I've always been impressed that he had enough faith in his readers to let them figure it out. They say, too, that Hemingway's adventures in Africa are a big influence on the large numbers of Americans who travel to Africa to safari and to climb Mt. Kilimanjaro; Stedman and others give him credit for inspiring so many Americans to dream about climbing that mountain in the middle of Africa.

I also read *The Shadow of Kilimanjaro—On Foot Across East Africa* by Rick Ridgeway and *Climbing Mount Kilimanjaro* by husband and wife team Stephen Carmichael and Susan Stoddard. The first is an engaging adventure story that I enjoyed, and the second is a well-documented description of the couple's climb, from details of their pre-climb workout, to health stats along the way. Uniquely different and worthwhile reads, the first is a longer story about bigger Africa, and the second an almost scientific approach to sharing what a climber might need to know to be prepared for their own adventure. I recommend them both.

WHAT TO WEAR

Yes, the question most people ask, especially every woman I've ever spoken to who is preparing for her own climb. I was determined to pack as lightly as I could—certainly didn't want to be carrying more than I needed and happy to avoid the dreaded stereotype of "the woman who packs too much." Not an easy goal considering that for this trip I would need three wardrobes: one for work in Burundi, one for climbing Mt. Kilimanjaro, and another for driving around in the Serengeti. It was, nonetheless, a challenge I was ready to meet!

It became a game to pack as lightly as possible—like a computer programmer who challenges herself to create a program with the fewest number of characters, like the haiku that allows for a limited and specific number of characters and syllables. The weight of everything mattered. Every item was evaluated for absolute purpose and need.

I knew from Heidrun that longer skirts and modest summer attire would be appropriate for Burundi. One pair of hollow-heeled, super-comfortable wedge sandals, two pencil skirts, one pair of khaki pants and a few interchangeable tops would do it (three shells, two over shirts, a light sweater and two white cotton tops). I selected two nice, lightweight scarves to serve as wraps/shawls or to wear around the neck for warmth, or simply a pretty accessory. Everything could be hand-washed and reused for safari if needed.

I chose simple, lightweight jewelry; two pair of earrings, two necklaces, a workhorse watch that was waterproof and not expensive. I did not wear my engagement ring but, as many women who travel know, it's wise to always wear a wedding ring. Even if you're not married. If you're not married, buy a cheap band for yourself and wear it to avoid any chance of appearing single; I've been told by women in-country and read that appearing single makes you a target for abuse.

Safari would be khakis, climbing pants, hiking boots, baseball cap (prime for sunshade), t-shirts, loose over-shirts, a fleece for morning rides and evening campfires. I'd have to re-wash the socks from climbing and maybe the pants.

Both Burundi and the Serengeti are malarial zones, and even though it was winter time in Africa, I took precautions with "Deep Woods Off" bug spray in a small, plastic pump container since, for this trip I was willing to go with Deet. I also discovered, through research, Permethrin insect repellent spray, which was outstanding: lasts for weeks and through several washings. After determining every item I'd be bringing with me, I assembled a moveable clothing rack outside, hung all of the items (except underwear and socks), then sprayed and dried every piece before packing it all up.

Colleagues in Burundi joked that the country is considered to be the mosquito capital of Africa, so despite the sprayed clothing, I did use the Deet spray twice daily in Burundi. I didn't need it on the mountain or on the Serengeti.

Packing for work in Burundi and safari in the Serengeti would be easy; it was deciding what to pack for the climb that would be the most important. I knew I'd need clothes that were tough and functional, both cool and warm. The best way to narrow this down would be—you guessed it—research.

WHAT TO PACK

I don't know for sure, but I'll bet if you asked anyone who's been there and back, one of the big questions they get from others planning to go is "What should I bring?" I asked the same question and here are some of the answers and my list (from memory). From my notes of the conversation with Linda Till:

Hiking boots—make sure they're broken in of course but even more importantly, you'll want extra footwear for a change up. Linda recommended an extra pair of slip on boots to give your feet a break, and also slippers to wear around camp—sturdy, slip on, warm. Think UGGs.

She recommended duct tape for blisters: if you see a blister forming, put duct tape on it and it'll help reduce the chance of it growing (who knew?). I didn't have the occasion to try this as I used second-skin type blister Band-Aids—more on those later—but I did carry a mini roll of duct tape in my backpack each day.

She reminded me of the importance of Gore-Tex pants and a jacket for inclement weather. I had both articles on my trip; thankfully never needed the pants and did wear the green jacket quite a lot because it was a work-horse outer layer for wind and you'll see it in a lot of the photos.

Me: *Would you have done anything differently?*

Linda: *Yes, I would have brought extra coats, outdoor coats. Even if you have to go to the Goodwill to buy them, bring whatever you can. One of the women in my group gave away the coat off her back and it moved me. I would have brought coats to give away.*

Linda recommended the four-part video series, *How To Prepare For Hiking Mt. Kilimanjaro* by LDGarber on YouTube, which I found to be very helpful, reinforcing what I'd read in Stedman, and heard from Linda and others.

Garber showed how he insulated his CamelBak tube and I think it was Garber who suggested that Kili climbers shouldn't bring a CameBak unless it's insulated. I will tell you that my water bottles froze overnight more than once, even inside my tent, but the CamelBak tube only froze on western breach morning. My guides advised it was okay to bring and use the CamelBak so I did, and the crew always melted the water in the frozen water bottles for me. I was able to drink from the water bottle on the way up the western breach until we met the sunshine and then the tube unfroze quickly, so fortunately it wasn't an issue. But I had excellent weather and that's something to consider since you never know what Mother Nature will bring to you.

Over dinner with new friends one evening I received some most excellent advice from Matt Friedman, a former personal trainer, who had summited Mt. Kilimanjaro the previous year. Now I'm guessing that Matt was an especially good trainer because he **listened** to what was working for me in my own training routine, to my questions, and he heard my concerns. His advice on training became my goal: "Deb, since you like the rotating stair machine (I call it The Gauntlet), set this goal: if you can climb 60 uninterrupted minutes at level 6, then you're ready and you will be able to handle the climb up Mt. Kilimanjaro." Matt also stressed the importance of warm gloves, telling me to bring my warmest pair. I was reminded of that advice on western breach morning when my hands were extremely cold because my gloves weren't even close to warm enough. I had two pair of Alan's gloves, one wool pair, and one Gore-Tex fleece pair. I've since found a pair of Nepalese yakwool gloves, fingerless with a mitten top that flips over them when you need to cover your fingertips. My guide Honest wore this type of glove which seemed to serve him well. I'd advise a liner glove as well.

I borrowed one of Mom's SPF hats. Mom lived at the seashore, in Wildwood, NJ, and had two floppy-type SPF50 hats. She gave one to me for this adventure, and it was invaluable because I have fair skin and the hat provided coverage for my scalp, ears, upper face and back of the neck. I bought shoelace-type string before I left and during the flight to Africa sewed it above the ears on each side so I could tie it down in the event of a windy day. I did need those ties. I had a UPenn baseball cap as well, providing effective shading for my eyes, and a conversation starter, too.

Outer layers included a polyfill vest, a waterproof shell with hood that could tie down around my face and an under layer of quicker-drying polyfill (vs. down which takes longer to dry if it gets wet). I wore the polyfill often at night because it was so soft, and used it often as a pillow. Two pair of hiking pants, one pair of wool pants (LOVED THESE!!) and rain pants. Carry the rain gear top/bottom with you in your day pack every day and maybe Murphy's Law will kick in for you like it did for me: if you have them and have them handy, you won't need them. I never wore the rain pants. Two lightweight wool shirts, one heavier wool shirt. One fleece. Underwear for each day plus one (they're light), two wool sports bras, wool socks enough to rotate for each day. One pair long wool underwear.

The dust does and will get into and all over everything, so just get used to it. And consider dark colors. My pretty pink long sleeved wool t-shirt was pretty grungy around the edges after a few days.

Snacks. Got to pack snacks. Costco makes a tasty trail mix with M&Ms that was a big hit with the whole porter team. They'll expand as you go up in altitude and you'll question the wisdom of bringing them when you feel their weight in comparison to the other items you have, but bring a lot and share them with your team; they sincerely appreciate it and you'll be glad you did.

Lip balm, sunscreen, and antibacterial ointment. Traumeel (odorless, clear homeopathic ointment for sore muscles). Cough drops—carry these in your day pack and bring enough to share; they come in handy on the dusty trail. I brought a cheap, light washcloth from the Dollar Store that I could leave behind if it got too grungy, and for me, I say forget those polypropylene 'trail towels' that don't absorb, I brought two real hand towels. The best thing for cleaning my body when there wasn't a shower around were, hands down, Wetnaps. One refill packet (without the hard plastic shell) may feel heavy and you'll doubt the wisdom of it if you're nutty about packed weight as I was, but every time I needed and used them, it affirmed the decision to bring them. One packet of 50 was more than enough for washing up every morning and evening on the trail, with bucket water and soap in between for feet, face and hands, or for use if your towelettes freeze (mine did not).

You will need a daypack and a big duffel; big huge plastic zip bags to store everything in; a sleeping bag and pad (unless you want to rent these but I'd much rather have my own and know it's clean).

I brought several ways to capture the experience—pen and paper, camera for video/audio/pictures and a miniature tape recorder, though in hindsight I could have used the 'Blair Witch' technique and just filmed myself talking but that would have been weird for me.

I did not bring novel reading. On purpose. I was determined to reduce distractions and focus only on my surroundings, and so I brought the whole Stedman book (trail bible) and read a small borrowed booklet Wilson shared with me on the flora and fauna of the mountain. I think it was a training booklet for guides. I read in my tent, by the light of a headlamp, usually at night before I went to sleep. The headlamp was useful in the evenings, especially on early morning walks to the bathroom, though I didn't need it every night thanks to the light of the full June moon and a clear sky.

WHAT I BROUGHT THAT I DIDN'T NEED OR USE AT ALL

The "Shewee" plastic funnel that allows a woman to pee standing up. Didn't like it, didn't use it, didn't need it.

A personal sleeping sheet. This was recommended by other travelers who'd been to bug-infested places around the world, and I thought for sure I'd need it but didn't. Never used it. Though I did learn from Dariya that she used hers as an extra insulating layer for warmth and I wish I'd thought of that.

WHAT I WOULD PACK, IF I WERE TO DO IT AGAIN

All of the above but in dark colors. Wool hat with earflaps and braided tie plus woolen glove/mitten pair, both of which I now own, and serious glove liners. I'd pack a few hand warmer packets, just a few (because they're extra weight and trash) and would use them just for the Western Breach morning.

I would have carried wrapped candies when walking around, to share with the Chagga kids and my crew. I would have brought more snacks to share. Warm pajamas—I packed shorts and a t-shirt then ended up wearing my wool clothes at night instead.

I unquestionably could have used *breathable SPF gloves* for the daytime to avoid sunburned hands and nails. I don't know if these exist but if you invent them, please let me know.

WHAT TO PACK IT IN

All that I'd read from SENE and others mentioned the need for a duffel bag for the trail. I found an Osprey bag, four feet tall and about the size of something that would cover a golf bag and then some. It was just what I needed. Tough nylon shell, long and padded loop for over-the-shoulder holding on, this was easy to maneuver and move through airports and the like. Held an amazing amount of stuff too: compressed sleeping bag, bed roll, three down coats, just about everything I would need for the climb.

I used a regular suitcase—large with 360 degree wheels and a handle, hard-sided—for the business and safari clothing and items.

My backpack was amazing. I had an old schoolbag type backpack that had travelled all around the world with me. It was a huge, bright blue thing with a massive main section, generous middle and convenient front with zip, mesh water bottle holders on each side and padded shoulder straps. I loved that bag.

I realized on a Patagonia hike in 2010, however, that this oldie-but-goodie wasn't going to cut it for the trip to Kilimanjaro. I perspired so much in Patagonia that I disintegrated more than one brown bag lunch stored in the main compartment of the pack.

I went to the new, local REI store to learn about and test out a few models, finally settling on an Osprey Stratos 24. It's relatively small—especially compared to the monster pack I'd been carrying—and I made the conscious choice to go with the smaller pack for this climb since

(a) I'd have the support of porters and,

(b) I believed the sales person when he suggested that if I had a bigger pack, I'd carry more.

It's roomy enough to hold my rain gear and supplies for day hikes and I'm sure I could loop a lot more onto it if needed. The front straps are padded with loops in just the right places including a clip-on loop for the spigot of my CamelBak, which nests nicely inside the larger section of the pack.

There is a lightweight aluminum frame inside that holds its shape and Super Bonus: the frame and taut, open-weave mesh layer form an air pocket for air flow around my back—what a gift that was on the trail!

There is more to the perfection of this pack that I hadn't experienced before: instead of tying around the waist, pulling on the shoulders and resting on the lower back, as my oldie-but-goodie pack did, THIS pack rests evenly on my hips with big, padded, wide straps.

This is the pack that inspires the "lioness walk" of confidence, born of free shoulders and an ergonomic design for maximum weight distribution.

I honestly do love this backpack.

May you enjoy your climb—*and*—have fun with it!

ABOUT THE AUTHOR

Deb Denis is an Executive Coach and Organizational Consultant who helps her clients blast through barriers to master more change than they previously thought possible. She's done this with hundreds of clients from all around the world and at varying levels within many industries.

Deb is Partner and Co-Founder of the Athena Project, LP (www.athenaproject.us), a firm focused on developing leaders, with particular expertise in developing women leaders to help businesses solve the "pipeline problem." In 2010 she founded Coaches Without Borders (www.coaches-without-borders.org), an international volunteer organization that pairs U.S.-trained Executive Coaches with leaders of aid organizations in Africa.

Deb loves to experience the world and has travelled, hiked and eaten on all six inhabited continents. Deb was born in Philadelphia, raised in upstate New York, and lives outside Philadelphia with her husband Alan and their golden retriever, Athena.

www.hersolosummit.com

www.debdenis.com

ABOUT MARION GRACE PUBLISHING

Marion Grace Publishing was established in 2012 as an independent book publisher. The company is named after the author's grandmother, Marion Grace Eckenroth, who was born in Lancaster, Pennsylvania. Marion was a daughter, sister, cousin, student, and later, an "Estee Lauder Girl" who loved going "down the shore."

Marion met her husband on Steel Pier in Atlantic City, where she saw the famous diving horse. She had three beautiful daughters who shared the initials SJS, and all the monogrammed sweaters that came after. She loved to take her daughters and grandchildren to Ocean City, New Jersey.

She was a teacher in the school district of Philadelphia during the mid-20th century and had a love of learning, all things cultural and her family. She loved animals and funded care for some via the Philadelphia Zoo and National Geographic Society. She had an appreciation for the finer things. She taught the next generations—her students and her family—about reading, writing and Philadelphia history.

Marion was born in 1910 and lived to see another century; she died in 2000.

MARION GRACE PUBLISHING

U.S.A.

WWW.MARIONGRACEPUBLISHING.COM

RECOMMENDED READING

In addition to the items listed in the bibliography, I recommend the following books, all stories of the mountain.

Carmichael, Stephen and Susan Stoddard. <u>Climbing Mt. Kilimanjaro</u>. 2nd edition. Medi-Ed Press. 2002.

Fitzpatrick, Mary. <u>Lonely Planet Tanzania</u>. 2008.

Hemingway, Ernest. <u>The Snows of Kilimanjaro and Other Stories</u>. Scribner. 1961.

Ridgeway, Rick. <u>The Shadow of Kilimanjaro—On Foot Across East Africa</u>. Owl Books. 1998.

Stedman, Henry. <u>Kilimanjaro—The Trekking Guide to Africa's Highest Mountain</u>. 3rd edition. 2010. If you only buy one, THIS IS THE BOOK

BIBLIOGRAPHY

Believe—The Words and Inspiration of Desmond Tutu. PQ Blackwell, Ltd., editor. Wild Dog Press. New Zealand. 2007.

Collins, Dr. Barbara. It's Your Turn, Find Your Authentic Self and Go Fetch It!. Self-published.

Green, Michael (illuminations) and Coleman Barks (translation). The Poetry of Rumi Journal. Brush Dance. San Rafael.

Hall, Judy. The Encyclopedia of Crystals. Godsfield Press/Octopus Publishing Group Ltd. London. 2007. Pages 214-15.

Mambo Mbalimbali—Tanzania Adventure Information. Summit Expedition and Nomadic Experience. PDF via email: tim@nomadicexperience.com. Updated March 2011.

Nepo, Mark. The Book of Awakening, Having the Life You Want by Being Present to the Life You Have. Conari Press. San Francisco. 2000. Pages 383-4.

Pasricha, Sarina (2012-06-13). Her Story: My Body is a Holocaust (Kindle Location 874). Kindle Edition.

Stedman, Henry. Kilimanjaro—The Trekking Guide to Africa's Highest Mountain. 3rd edition. 2010.

www.authentichappiness.com. VIA Signature Survey Results (personal). 2009.

www.davestravelcorner.com/journals/publish/article_21.shtml. Accessed February 2011.

www.frontiersoftravel.com. Image: Trail map of Mt. Kilimanjaro. Accessed March, 2012.

www.ultimatekilimanjaro.com/preparation.htm. Accessed February 2011.

www.wegoingup.com. Accessed May 2012.

www.westernbreach.co.uk/route.html. Western Breach Safety Report. Accessed May, 2012.

Made in the USA
San Bernardino, CA
03 November 2013